MUSIC IN AMERICAN LIFE

Books in the series:

Git Along, Little Dogies

GIT ALONG, LITTLE DOGIES

SONGS AND SONGMAKERS
OF THE AMERICAN WEST

JOHN I. WHITE

with a Foreword by Austin E. Fife

UNIVERSITY OF ILLINOIS PRESS

Urbana   Chicago   London

Library of Congress Cataloging in Publication Data

White, John Irwin, 1902–
    Git along, little dogies.

    (Music in American life)
    Bibliography and discography: p.
    "A John White discography": p.
    Includes index.
    1. Music, Popular (Songs, etc.)—The West—History
and criticism.   2. Cowboys—Songs and music—History
and criticism.   3. Musicians—The West.   I. Title.
ML3551.W48   784.4′978   75—6704
ISBN 0–252–00327–6

Grateful acknowledgment is made for permission to use the following material.

"Whoopee Ti Yi Yo, Git Along Little Dogies," "The Big Corral," and "Great Grandad" from *The Lonesome Cowboy: Songs of the Plains and Hills* by John White and George Shackley (New York: Al Piantadosi, 1929). By special permission of the publisher, Jerry Vogel Music Co., Inc.

"The Railroad Corral" from *This Is Music*, Book VI, by William R. Sur, Robert E. Nye, William R. Fisher, and Mary E. Tolbert (Boston: Allyn and Bacon, 1962). Copyright 1967 and 1962 by Allyn and Bacon, Inc. Used by permission.

"Night Herding Song" from *Songs of the American West* by Richard E. Lingenfelter, Richard A. Dwyer, and David Cohen (Berkeley and Los Angeles: University of California Press, 1968). Reprinted by permission of The Regents of the University of California.

"The Grass of Uncle Sam" from *Songs of the Open Range* by Ina Sires (Boston: C. C. Birchard & Co., 1928). Copyright 1928 by C. C. Birchard & Co. Copyright renewed. All rights reserved. Used by permission.

"The Sierry Petes (or, Tying the Knots in the Devil's Tail)," "The Moonshine Steer," and "The Dude Wrangler" from *Orejana Bull for Cowboys Only* by Gail I. Gardner (4th printing, Phoenix: Messenger Printing Co., 1965). Copyright 1935. Copyright renewed 1963. Used by permission.

"The Glory Trail," "Ridin'," and "A Cowboy's Prayer" from *Sun and Saddle Leather* by Charles Badger Clark (1915; revised, Stockton, Calif.: Westerners Foundation, 1962). Copyright by Westerners International. Reproduced by special permission.

"The Strawberry Roan" from *Those Fabulous "Beverly Hill Billies,"* Rare Arts Records WLP 1000. By permission of Stanley Floyd Kilarr.

"Great Grandma" from *Americans and Their Songs* by Frank Luther (New York and London: Harper & Brothers, 1942). Copyright by Frank Luther. Used by permission.

To my wife, Augusta

who felt that this book should be dedicated
to the late Romaine Lowdermilk, from whom I
heard my first cowboy song, in 1924, and to
Harlan Daniel, who forty years later convinced
me that I was a link with the past and for
posterity's sake I should do something about it

Contents

Foreword

A century has passed during which cowboy and western songs have been created, sung, and handed down among three or four generations of settlers in the plains and intermountain states, and, in fact, throughout the length and breadth of the land. Some of these songs show a servile dependency on British folk and popular songs of the eighteenth and nineteenth centuries. Others, using stylistic and metrical devices true and tested in the English language for five hundred years or more, deal largely with New World people, places, and circumstances.

Cowboy songs made their appearance in the early 1870s, sung first on ranches and in settlements on the Great Plains where cattle trail and railroad met. In the eighties and nineties texts began to appear also in plains and western newspapers, in farm and cattlemen's magazines, and even in a few periodicals distributed nationwide. New technological devices and arrangements for their use brought publisher, singer, and fan even closer together: song folios and sheet music, acoustical recordings on cylinders and 78 rpm records before World War I; radio, movies, electronic recordings, and television thereafter.

For a long time critics of the academic variety—"folklorists," that is—went on with their research as if these technological devices did not exist. To be worthy of their interest a song had to have trans-Atlantic roots or resemble closely songs that did. It had to come down through oral tradition. It had to originate as, or become through progressive transformations, the communal expression of a "folk," "ethnic," or other group. For their documentation folklorists relied mostly upon collections made from oral sources and published in journals of folklore or in books by and for educated people. Their work was thus enormously simplified, as were their conclusions, since a whole aspect of the life of folk and popular songs was being ignored: songs, for example, that reached millions of listeners in a few short weeks on 78 rpm records, or instantaneously through radio networks. Cowboy and western songs were available to thousands of buffs through song folios from ten to seventy pages in size, containing text, melody, and piano arrangement or tablature, and costing a dollar or less. Like the minstrels of ancient times, vaudeville artists and revivalist singing groups infiltrated the West, singing traditional and new popular songs in fundamentalist churches, labor union assembly halls, and commercially operated theaters. The lore of sailor, lumberjack, prospector, sodbuster, Indian, Mexican American, black, and cowboy was sung and strummed to listeners everywhere. From about 1910 the new mass media brought these songs to millions of listeners who, in an earlier day, could not have been reached. Songs like "Home on the Range," "The Streets of Laredo," or "The Big Rock Candy Mountain" were planted in the minds of people as "memory bank" companions to the national anthem and popular hymns.

Not only did the academic folklorists tend to shun these marvelous new arrangements for the dissemination of songs, but they were also generally not curious about authorship or cautious about giving credit when it was due—so many false claims to authorship had been made. The authors themselves had contributed to the befuddlement: Jack Thorp printed "Little Joe the Wrangler" without credit to himself in his memorable 1908 booklet of cowboy songs. Gail Gardner filed no copyright on "Tying the Knots in the Devil's Tail," written in 1917, until 1935, when it angered him to see it in print and copyrighted by "Powder River" Jack Lee. How could a Curley Fletcher anticipate, as he sent his "Strawberry Roan" to the *Arizona Record* at Globe, where it was first printed on December 16, 1915, that later it would sell a few million 78 rpm records, appear in scores of song folios and other books, and provide the makings of a movie script? He even ended up paying royalties for the right to publish a tune and refrain for his own song! When a song gets caught in a tidal wave like the cult for the American cowboy no finger can thereafter plug the hole in the dike on behalf of its author.

John I. White is not an academic folklorist, though articles by him have appeared in scholarly journals of folklore, music, and history. He is not a working cowboy, though ranch people have heard him sing by radio and by phonograph the songs they claimed as their own, or have learned their cowboy and western songs from folios edited by him. White is not even a yodelling, guitar-strumming dude riding herd around studio folk rather than around the range dogies, though for several years as the Lonesome Cowboy his voice was beamed across the land. He has written and published articles about a score or more of the cowboy and western songs he liked the best. In this book he has brought together several of these studies, along with essays not published heretofore.

From the early thirties onward he has maintained systematic files on nearly all the manifestations of cowboy and western songs in our culture: card files on songs sung by him during his radio days (1926–36) and on other western songs; bibliographical files on books containing "more than one or two western songs" and on magazine and newspaper articles concerning them. "My thickest files," he says, "are largely about people—western songmakers whom I either knew or corresponded with way back when . . . Badger Clark . . . Curley Fletcher, D. J. O'Malley, [Romaine] Lowdermilk, Will Barnes, Joseph Mills Hanson, Owen Wister"—and on other people connected in whatever way with cowboy and western music. Finally, he has separate manila folders on individual songs: "catch-all folders," he calls them, "containing anything I run across concerning these songs."

The essays that follow reflect White's close friendships and lively correspondence; they reveal how faithful has been his memory and how carefully he has gone about his research. He has established time, place, and circumstance of a song's origin, often determining its authorship and establishing its role in the evolution of the popular song tradition of Anglo-America. This work will enlighten many aspects of the important role played by cowboy and western songs in American life.

AUSTIN E. FIFE

Just for the Record

For those unacquainted with the author of this book, any explanation of how it came to be written and my qualifications for writing it must, of necessity, include considerable personal information extending back over a good many years.

Born and raised in a musical family at Washington, D.C., I attended the University of Maryland at College Park, where my major was English and my principal extra-curricular activities involved the college newspaper, the glee club, and tooting a clarinet in the ROTC band. My graduation present from my parents was a trip to Arizona, where I spent the summer of 1924. There I had numerous cousins and, most important of all, a brother, Lewis Cass White, who had located in Wickenburg and counted among his friends a rancher named Romaine H. Lowdermilk.

Romaine, a bachelor of thirty-four, lived with his widowed mother, on land he had homesteaded, and operated a one-man cattle outfit. On the side he contributed a weekly column of alleged wit and wisdom to a Prescott newspaper and wrote western adventure stories for the pulp magazines. Moreover, at the drop of a ten-gallon hat he would entertain any passing visitor with a guitar and a seemingly inexhaustible supply of cowboy songs. When he tired of singing, he would sometimes unlimber a lasso and vary the program with an exhibition of rope twirling, once in a while walking a tightwire at the same time.

As I recall it, my brother and I spent about two weeks at Romaine's Kay-El-Bar Ranch beside the dry bed of the Hassayampa River, fascinated by his talents. While I never mastered the rope or the tightwire, I

1

must say I did rather well with the music. I, too, had a fair collection of songs, most of them new to Romaine, that I rendered to the accompaniment of a ukulele. As we sat around the corral or in the shade of the mesquite trees, we amused each other trading ballads. Our host also introduced us to a dog-eared copy of the first John A. Lomax anthology, *Cowboy Songs and Other Frontier Ballads*. Greatly impressed, I purchased one at the earliest opportunity. I also resolved to acquire a guitar the minute I returned home.

Accordingly, I was soon entertaining my friends and relatives back East with those wonderful old western ditties I had first heard on Romaine's ranch. In fact, that became my avocation. For a vocation, with the help of a friend on the inside, I landed a job on the sports desk of the Washington *Star*. But after nearly two years of writing about high school athletic contests and saving my money, I decided to enroll in the graduate school at Columbia University in New York. Naturally the guitar went along. I was to find that the instrument and my newly acquired songs of the range would open a good many doors.

One day on the street, late in 1926, I encountered an old friend, a professional singer. Over a cup of coffee he told me he performed on the radio. When I asked what *I* had to do to get on the air, he replied: "Just write to the program manager of NBC station WEAF at 195 Broadway and ask for an audition."

"Is it that easy?" I asked in disbelief.

"That's right. If you have anything at all, it's that simple," he concluded, giving me the gentleman's name.

In those days it *was* that simple. I followed his advice, and in a week or so, my letter of invitation in my pocket and the guitar case under my arm, I knocked on NBC's door, to be greeted by a smiling receptionist.

"What do *you* do?"

"Why, I sing cowboy songs, and I have an appointment for an audition."

"Good-ee!" she beamed. "I just *love* cowboy songs! Come on in!"

The program manager's office was just large enough for his desk and chair and a sofa. As I unpacked the guitar I noticed the receptionist slip in and sit down. I perched on the edge of the desk and sang two or three songs.

"Do you have a lot of those?" the gentleman asked.

"Why yes, I do," I replied, preparing to uncork a few more.

But he held up his hand and turned to the girl. "Well, what do you think?"

"I think he's great!"

Romaine Lowdermilk proves his versatility by spinning a rope while walking a tightwire.

The author entertains his brother Luke at Wickenburg, Arizona, 1933.

Left to right: Romaine Lowdermilk, the author, and a brother, L. C. "Bob" White, 1924.

The author, 1930.

"Well, put him on."

Right there I learned never to underestimate the power of a woman.

Putting me on, in 1926, meant that I could sing and talk about my songs for fifteen minutes one afternoon a week, *for fun*. That was a bit discouraging, but one has to start somewhere. So I started.

When I went to the station for my second session I was surprised, in fact thrilled, to discover that my debut on the airwaves had generated at least half a dozen fan letters. In fifteen minutes I could sing only three songs, possibly four if I hurried, but my listeners seemed to like the little they had heard.

This "for free" arrangement continued for several months. However, during this time NBC did work me into an evening program or two that ended my amateur status; I actually got paid for singing. Then I had a call from the manager of station WOR, who offered me twenty-five dollars for doing the same thing I had been doing for love at WEAF. Shortly after I moved to WOR I took a full-time job with General Drafting Company, a firm supplying maps and routing services to several

4

large oil companies. Although this was to have been a summer engagement, it continued for thirty-eight years. The radio work, which lasted almost ten years on a once-a-week basis, was strictly a moonlighting operation.

At WOR I did my fifteen-minute solo act for a while before being teamed up with a male quartet specializing in old favorites like "Won't You Come Home, Bill Bailey?" and chiming in on the choruses of my western numbers. Billed as the Lone Star Rangers, we made personal appearances, too. When the annual rodeo came to town in the fall of 1928 we even dressed up in rented cowboy costumes and sang from a box at Madison Square Garden. Somewhere along the way I acquired the nickname "The Lonesome Cowboy."

WOR's musical director, George Shackley, suggested that he and I do a folio of western songs. This publication—*The Lonesome Cowboy: Songs of the Plains and Hills*—was issued in 1929 by Al Piantadosi (New York). It consisted of twenty numbers, with piano accompaniment. In addition to old favorites that had been available to folksingers since the first Lomax collection was printed in 1910, we included two based on poems by E. A. Brininstool for which Romaine Lowdermilk had made up good tunes. These were "Trouble for the Range Cook," describing the problems that arise when the chuck wagon gets stuck in the mud, and "His Trademarks," whose punch line is "He sticks to his old sombrero, he sticks to his high-heeled boots." The folio also had three complete strangers—"Great Grandad," "Great Grandma," and "The Big Corral," each of which has its own chapter in this book.

In addition to getting my name on a published song folio, in the same year, by sheer happenstance, I became what is commonly known as "a recording artist." Arthur Satherley of New York's American Record Corporation needed a hillbilly singer and asked Roy Smeck, known in the entertainment world as the Wizard of the Strings, if he knew one. Although only a casual acquaintance, Roy somehow felt that I might qualify, so he took me around. I passed inspection, but before becoming a hillbilly singer I talked Satherley into letting me start with "Great Grandad" and "The Little Old Sod Shanty on the Claim." Then ARC began giving me hillbilly numbers written in Tin Pan Alley and songs which Vernon Dalhart had recorded elsewhere but for legal reasons was not permitted to sing for Satherley's company. Somehow my heart wasn't in it. But before the windup, in 1931, I did manage to record "The Strawberry Roan" and "Whoopee Ti Yi Yo, Git Along, Little Dogies."

Altogether I recorded twenty songs (two of these were variants of

"The Strawberry Roan"), all of which were issued on 78 rpm discs.[1] Since Roy Smeck got me the job, he supplied guitar accompaniment, although on the air I had always played my own. We split evenly. As we normally made two sides at a session, we each received seventy-five dollars for a morning's work. Fortunately, at General Drafting I had an indulgent boss who didn't mind my slipping away for a morning once every two or three months to add to my income.

Old newspaper clippings show that in the spring of 1930 the Lonesome Cowboy was back at NBC, now installed in fine new studios at Radio City, supplying musical background for a once-a-week dramatic series titled "Frontier Days." Like virtually every other show I had been involved with on radio, this was a "sustaining program," one put on by the station without commercial sponsorship and, consequently, not making me rich.

One day two emissaries from the McCann-Erickson advertising agency showed up at the studio and said they would like to engage me as both singer and narrator on a thirty-minute coast-to-coast network dramatic show called "Death Valley Days," to be sponsored by the Pacific Coast Borax Company and scheduled to start in the fall of 1930. I pointed out that I was not an actor and, furthermore, because of my regular daytime job I would not be able to attend rehearsals. Besides, I told them, I planned to get married soon to my long-time sweetheart in Washington, Augusta Postles, and had even considered giving up entertaining in order to devote full time to being a good husband.

They compromised on the spot, and it was arranged that I would do just my specialty—sing western numbers between the acts of the play. They would mail me a script a week in advance. I would send in a list of appropriate songs for copyright check, then report for dress rehearsal each Tuesday night an hour before the show went on the air This idyllic arrangement, which included receiving a generous check each week, lasted nearly six years. After that, increasing responsibilities connected with my daytime work made it necessary for me to retire permanently from the professional entertainment field. Somehow, the "Death Valley Days" radio show got along without me until 1941; then it was dropped. In 1951 it was revived for television and a new episode aired once a week for twenty years. Reruns are still being shown in many United States cities, also in foreign markets.

Appearing on a big network station was most enjoyable while it lasted. In winter the male members of our Wild West show wore tuxedos, the ladies evening dresses, as we performed before large studio audiences. The only inconvenience I can recall was having to interrupt the honeymoon to be on hand for the second show. Because

20 MULE TEAM BORAX
SOFTENS WATER SAFELY

In contrast to the many harsh water softeners, 20 Mule Team Borax is a mild but effective water softener and is safe to use for the most delicate fabrics and will not injure the hands.

20 Mule Team Borax aids the soap to do a more efficient cleaning job for all household purposes: dishwashing, laundry, woodwork, refrigerator. It cleans, deodorizes and leaves everything hygienically sweet and fresh.

A little 20 Mule Team Borax sprinkled around the kitchen sink, in crevices and corners, will banish all kinds of household insect pests. It is non-poisonous and safe to use.

Directions for the general use of 20 Mule Team Borax are printed right on the package. Get a package from your grocer or druggist and demonstrate its practical efficiency to your own satisfaction.

PACIFIC COAST BORAX COMPANY
2295 LUMBER STREET, CHICAGO, ILL.
51 MADISON AVE., NEW YORK, N. Y.
WILMINGTON, CALIF.

The "Old Ranger" and The "Lonesome Cowboy" *broadcasting*

Thrilling and Dramatic Stories in and around
"DEATH VALLEY"

Be sure to listen in and hear the popular "Old Ranger" relate the interesting and entertaining stories in the "Death Valley Days" radio program. The stories are based upon actual happenings and historical facts; tales of the early pioneer days, the days of '49, the emigrant, the prospector and the famous 20 Mule Team drivers.

Supporting the "Old Ranger" is John White, the "Lonesome Cowboy" who strums his guitar and sings the songs of the cattle trail and wide open spaces.

It is now over three years since the combined attraction of the "Old Ranger" and the "Lonesome Cowboy" first went on-the-air in the "Death Valley Days" radio program over a vast network of NBC stations. Its popularity is greater than ever before.

Listen in —
EVERY THURSDAY NIGHT
8:00- 8:30 Central Standard Time

STATIONS

WLS	Chicago
KSO	Des Moines
KWCR	Cedar Rapids
KOIL	Council Bluffs
KWK	St. Louis
WREN	Kansas City
WLW	Cincinnati

"Death Valley Days" radio program is sponsored by the manufacturers of the well-known 20 Mule Team brand of Borax, on sale at your grocer or druggist.

20 MULE TEAM BORAX

Advertising flyer, 1930.

Radio Star Weds

—Herald Staff Photo

THE "LONESOME COWBOY," John I. White, and his bride, the former Miss Augusta Postles, as they left the Church of St. Stephen and the Incarnation yesterday afternoon.

"Lonesome Cowboy Lassoed" might well have been the caption for this picture printed in the Washington, D.C., *Herald* on Sunday, October 5, 1930, five days after the first airing of "Death Valley Days." It shows the author and his bride, the former Augusta Braxton Postles, leaving the Washington church in which they were married.

9

of the time lag in the West, for a short period the program was rebroad-cast live from New York three hours later. But soon it was being aired from San Francisco also, with a different cast of actors and a singer named Charles Marshall.

The stories our group dramatized were more or less true incidents that had happened in Death Valley, where, half a century before, highly valuable borax was mined and hauled out to civilization in sturdy wagons pulled by the famous twenty-mule teams, or that had occurred in adjacent areas of southern California or Nevada. Strangely enough, most of the scripts were written by a woman, the late Ruth Cornwall Woodman, a Vassar graduate and mother of two children. For authenticity, Mrs. Woodman traveled from her home in Rye, New York, to the southwestern desert at least once a year, sometimes twice, for *fourteen* years to fraternize with grizzled prospectors and former muleskinners and to interview such picturesque characters as Death Valley Scotty, who drove around with a machine-gun mounted on the front of his car and lived in a "castle" that has since become a tourist attraction in Death Valley National Monument. Shortly before she passed away in 1970, this amazing lady told me she had written some 750 half-hour radio scripts for "Death Valley Days," which doesn't include her work on the later television presentations.

While the Lonesome Cowboy was performing on "Death Valley Days," the gossip columnists had a merry time debunking him.

One Nellie Revell wrote in *Radio Digest* for January, 1932: "John White is neither a cowboy, nor is he lonesome. I must admit, though, that he certainly sounds that way over the radio when he strums his guitar and sings those plaintive ballads of the Western trails. However, John can claim to be a synthetic cowboy. He once spent a summer on a dude ranch in Arizona, but the nearest he ever came to milking a cow was to open a can of condensed milk. Moreover, The Lonesome Cowboy doesn't even look like a cowboy. He's a dapper, smooth-shaven 'city feller' type of man still in his twenties. What's more, instead of spurs, he wears spats." [2]

Frank Zahner, radio commentator for the *Newark Sunday Ledger*, put his tongue in his cheek and contributed the following on March 27, 1932: "John don't know the diff between a maverick and four hoofs of pedigreed stock . . . never rode range or handled a branding iron . . . yet he does hand out a brand of range songs that agot all the ol' top-hands hogtied. Thar he sits on a high stool close up to the mike . . . he's a-singin' in a rich baritone voice . . . singin' like the old cowboys would have liked to have done . . . he's ridin' herd all over a big guitar . . . that's the twang of the old West in his voice . . . you can smell the

Cowboy Songs

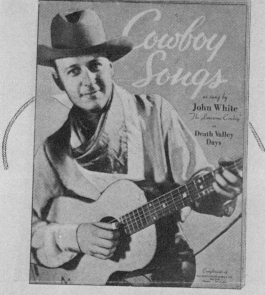

Send a 20 Mule Team Borax top for this book

COWBOY songs are fun to sing—and fun to collect! Here's a special collection of six of the songs John White (The Lonesome Cowboy) has made famous on the Death Valley Days' radio programs. This fascinating song book is yours in exchange for a 20 Mule Team Borax box top. Send for it today!

Real cowboy songs . . . real Western twang . . . and real Western tales make each Death Valley Days' sketch a half hour of fast-moving fun, adventure and romance. This popular program is broadcast Thursday nights at 7 P. M. Central Standard Time over stations WLW, WLS, WJZ and KWK.

Don't miss this radio treat each week. And let 20 Mule Team Borax lighten your work washday and everyday. Right now 20 Mule Team can help you keep your summer cottons bright and gay . . . your linens white and fresh. Use Borax, too, to keep the refrigerator sweet and clean. Sprinkle it around if ants find their way to your bread box. And try a teaspoonful in the dishpan—Borax cuts grease, makes soap go further and glass and china sparkle.

All pure Borax. You'll find it pays to ask for 20 MULE TEAM by name. For many "borax compounds" are sold today that contain very little Borax. Some of them as little as 5%. 20 Mule Team is *all* pure Borax — that's why it is such an indispensable household aid.

Use this coupon

Pacific Coast Borax Company
51 Madison Avenue, New York, N. Y.
I am attaching a 20 Mule Team Borax Box Top. Please send me in exchange your book of Cowboy Songs.

Name . . . .
Address . . . .
City . . . . State . . . .
H. S.

From *Holland's, the Magazine of the South,*
September, 1934, p. 41.

Scenes from Death Valley

Principals in the Cast of the Death Valley Days Dramas heard Over an NBC-WJZ Network. At the Top Left is Tim Frawley, the "Old Ranger". Beside Him is Peggy Allenby, Leading Lady, and Below, Left to Right, are Jack McBride, Character Actor, and John White, the Lonesome Cowboy.

New York, May 26.—A long period of research into the lore of one of the most desolate spots in the United States—Death Valley in California—preceded the initial presentation of Death Valley Days over a National Broadcasting Company network in the fall of 1930.

It began with the discovery of the arid valley by whites, parts of a wagon train headed for California and gold, whose survivors gave the valley its name and were later themselves known to history as the Bennet Arcane party.

Death Valley is now a national preserve, boasting excellent motor roads and a modern inn, but the modern age has in no way dimmed the tragic romance of the weird spot, 300 feet below sea level, where bottomless salt marshes might still swallow the unwary, and whose romance still lives in the series heard each Thursday at 8 p. m. over an NBC-WJZ network.

From the Saint Petersburg, Florida, *Tribune*, May 27, 1933.

The author, 1933.

sagebrush . . . doggone it . . . he agot me brushin' the alkali sand off my chaps."

Radio Guide once referred to me as "John White, the bank clerk who is known in the radio world as The Lonesome Cowboy." Author Albert Payson Terhune, when pinch-hitting for the regular radio columnist on the *New York Evening Journal*, wrote: " 'Death Valley Days' with its drugstore cowboy, John White, holds me as tightly as did 'Deadwood Dick' in my childhood."[3]

While on radio, particularly during the "Death Valley Days" period, I spent a great deal of time researching the songs I was singing. My aim was to sound as genuine as possible. In addition to fine-combing the New York Public Library and buying every old songbook I could find, I corresponded with people all over the country with a special interest in American folksong—among them John A. Lomax, J. Frank Dobie, Will Barnes, Joseph Mills Hanson, Badger Clark, Owen Wister. On a trip to Death Valley I detoured via Wisconsin to see cowboy poet D. J. O'Malley; the result, a twenty-page, privately printed pamphlet about O'Malley's life and verses. Several newspaper and magazine articles on old songs also carried my name. I kept in touch with Romaine Lowdermilk. In 1932 I wrote Gail Gardner at Prescott, Arizona, for permission to sing his famous ditty "Tying the Knots in the Devil's Tail" and also to make sure I had the official version.

Shortly after I dropped out of radio, in 1936, to give full time to the map business and a growing family, all this correspondence was filed away. It probably was not touched until nearly thirty years later, when I received a long-distance telephone call that prompted me to look through it again. The caller was a stranger to me, a Chicago record collector named Harlan Daniel, who seemed to know more about my past than I did. He had all of my recordings, which was more than I could say. He had several projects going and needed some of the information I apparently had stashed away long ago.

In searching for what Harlan wanted, I came to realize I had a unique collection of data on the subject of western songs that some day would go out with the trash unless I did something about it. As I would soon be retiring from business, I put this at the top of the list of things to be taken care of when I no longer had to report to an office each morning.

On September 30, 1965, I cleared off my desk at General Drafting Company. After enjoying a bit of travel, I set up shop as a free-lance writer of magazine articles. *Montana* printed my first offering, the story of Owen Wister's famed novel *The Virginian*, which had come into the world the same month that I did and is still very much on the active list. Then I buckled down to writing about western songs and the people who wrote them, starting with a piece on Gail Gardner for the Sunday supplement of the *Arizona Republic* (Phoenix), for May 7, 1967. Three others with Arizona settings were written for the same publication, another for *Arizona Highways*.

Two articles appeared in the *Journal of American Folklore*, three in *Western Folklore. Montana* ran the biographical sketch of D. J.

O'Malley that forms the lengthiest chapter in this book. And so it went. My list shows nineteen published articles on songs of the West.

In the summer of 1972, out of the blue, I received a letter from the University of Illinois Press asking whether I would consider putting most of these articles in a book, one of a new series called Music in American Life. To say that I felt honored is putting it mildly.

Producing such a volume hasn't been as simple as getting on the radio. There were new chapters to be written, old ones to be revised. And, as with any project of this nature, there were what seemed like hundreds of loose ends to be pulled together. But it, too, has been great fun. I hope that you will get as much enjoyment out of the reading as I did from the writing.

Six chapters were prepared especially for the book: "Owen Wister, Songwriter," "Singin' to 'em," "Move Slow, Dogies, Move Slow," "Where the Deer and the Antelope Play," " 'The Little Old Sod Shanty on the Claim,' " and "Two Pioneer Collectors."

In the pages that follow I have not attempted to run the gamut of western songs. In general, I have written only about those I used to enjoy singing and still do, for that matter, which encompasses a fairly broad field at that. With the exception of "Home on the Range," in which I had a personal stake some forty years ago, I have not dwelt on songs that have been discussed at length by others, for example "Oh, Bury Me Not on the Lone Prairie" and "The Cowboy's Lament." However, for the benefit of readers new to western folksong, these titles appear in the Index with references to footnotes explaining where data concerning them may be found.

I wish to express my thanks to all those who supplied illustrations, permitted me to use previously published material, or otherwise aided me in the work. Special thanks go to Judith McCulloh, who thought of the book in the first place and, in the second place, helped guide me through the maze of detail involved in my first major publishing venture.

NOTES

1. For details see the discography in Appendix B.
2. *Radio Digest*, Jan., 1932, p. 53.
3. *Radio Guide*, Oct. 31, 1931; *New York Evening Journal*, July 28, 1934.

1

"Git Along, Little Dogies"

As I was a-walk-ing one morn-ing for plea-sure I

spied a cow-punch-er a-rid-ing a-long. His

hat was throwed back and his spurs was a-jin-gling And

as he ap-proach'd me was sing-ing this song.

CHORUS

Whoop-ee ti-yi-yo, git a-long, lit-tle do-gies It's

your mis-for-tune and none of my own Whoop-

16

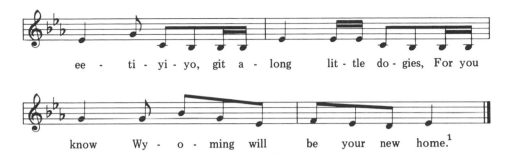

ee - ti - yi - yo, git a - long lit - tle do - gies, For you

know Wy - o - ming will be your new home.[1]

The long-forgotten western diaries of Owen Wister, author of *The Virginian*, contribute an interesting bit to the history of one of the best-known American cowboy songs—one usually titled "Whoopee Ti Yi Yo, Git Along, Little Dogies"—and indicate that more than three-quarters of a century ago Texas cowpunchers were familiar with this lyrical description of life on the cattle trail.[2]

Beginning in 1885, when he made his first trip from his home in Philadelphia to Wyoming in search of health and big game, Wister kept careful records of his many western journeys—in fifteen pocket-size notebooks now at the Western History Research Center in the University of Wyoming Library. In 1952, long after his death and fifty years after the publication of his famous novel (still available in numerous editions), these diaries were found in Wister's old writing desk, where they had reposed for sixty-odd years. His daughter, Fanny Kemble Wister (Mrs. Walter Stokes), undertook the task of editing them, and in 1958 they were published by the University of Chicago Press in a delightful volume called *Owen Wister Out West: His Journals and Letters*.

The journal for February-March, 1893, has the following entry written at Brownwood in central Texas: "I have come upon a unique song . . . and I transcribe it faithfully. Only a cowboy could have produced such an effusion. It has the earmark of entire genuineness." Wister then carefully wrote out these stanzas:

> As I walked out one morning for pleasure,
> I met a cowpuncher a-jogging along.
> His hat was thrown back and his spurs was a-jingling,
> And as he advanced he was singing this song.
>
>> Sing hooplio get along my little dogies,
>> For Wyoming shall be your new home.
>> Its hooping and yelling and cursing those dogies
>> To our misfortune but none of your own.

Photographed here in 1887 at a studio in Yellowstone National Park, twenty-seven-year-old Owen Wister was still to become famous as the author of *The Virginian* and numerous other tales with "cattle land" as their setting. Photograph courtesy of Western History Research Center, University of Wyoming.

In the Springtime we round up the dogies,
Slap on the brands and bob off their tails.
Then we cut herd and herd is inspected,
And then we throw them on the trail.

   Chorus:

In the evening we round in the dogies
As they are grazing from herd all around.
You have no idea the trouble they give us
As we are holding them on the bedground.

   Chorus:

In the morning we throw off the bedground,
Aiming to graze them an hour or two.
When they are full, you think you can drive them
On the trail, but be damned if you do.

   Chorus:

Some fellows go on the trail for pleasure,
But they have got this thing down wrong.
If it hadn't bin for these troublesome dogies,
I never would thought of writing this song.

   Chorus: [3]

Another noted writer on the West, Andy Adams, appears to have been the first actually to mention "Whoopee Ti Yi Yo" in print, in *The Log of a Cowboy*, published in 1903, just a year after Wister's novel *The Virginian* came out. Adams does little more than barely mention it, but the two lines he quotes are obviously from the same song. Near the end of his classic description of cowboy life in the 1880s (which also is still in print) he tells of pushing a trail herd on a forced march by moonlight: ". . . someone in the lead wig-wagged his lantern; it was answered by the light in the rear, and the next minute the old rear song,—

> Ip-e-la-ago, go along little doggie,
> You'll make a beef steer by-and-by,—

reached us riders in the swing, and we knew the rear guard of cattle was being pushed forward." [4]

How can the spelling "doggie" instead of the usual "dogie" be explained? Very likely it was the error of a typesetter who never had heard young steers called "dogies," with a long *o*. Adams himself, in fact, didn't call them that. Throughout his fascinating fictional account of the hardships and dangers encountered while driving a herd twenty-five hundred miles from southern Texas to an Indian reservation in northern Montana he invariably spoke of "the cattle" or "the herd," never of "the dogies." [5]

Just six weeks before this trail herd of shaggy Longhorn beeves appeared in the October 19, 1867, *Harper's Weekly*, a new era had begun as twenty cars loaded with similar animals from Texas left the newly established railhead at Abilene, Kansas, bound for Chicago. That fall some thirty-five thousand steers came bawling into Abilene, the start of a veritable flood of beef-on-the-hoof that moved north from the Lone Star State every summer for the next two decades, before barbwire and farming homesteads blocked the great cattle trails.

Out West for March, 1908, was a bit more generous than author Andy Adams. Readers of an article by Sharlot M. Hall, "Old Range Days and New in Arizona," found ten lines addressed to the little dogies, captioned "Old Trail-song of the 'Eighties."

> Get along, get along, little dogie,
> You're going to be a beef-steer by-and-by.
> Your mother she was raised way down in Texas,
> Where the jimson weed and sand-burrs grow;
> Now we'll fill you up on prickly pear and cholla,
> Till you're ready for the trail to Idaho.
> Oh! you'll be soup for Uncle Sam's Injuns;
> It's "Beef, heap beef" you hear 'em cry;
> Get along, get along, little dogie,
> For the Injuns they'll eat you by-and-by.[6]

It was the famous ballad hunter and folklorist John Avery Lomax who first made the song "Whoopee Ti Yi Yo" available to the general public. He included a version with seven stanzas and many variations from Wister's in his pioneer collection *Cowboy Songs and Other Frontier Ballads*, issued in 1910. This was the first book of native American folksongs that also contained music, in this case tunes captured in cow camps, saloons, or any other place the indomitable professor from Texas could persuade a singer to face his crude recording machine. Unfortunately, the New York publisher of this first Lomax book saw fit to publish music for only eighteen of more than a hundred songs that had been recorded. "Whoopee Ti Yi Yo" was among the lucky eighteen. Lomax included a stanza with lines similar to those used by Andy Adams and Sharlot M. Hall and a chorus with a slightly different twist from the one preserved by Wister.

> Oh, you'll be soup for Uncle Sam's Injuns;
> "It's beef, heap beef," I hear them cry.
> Git along, git along, git along little dogies
> You're going to be beef steers by and by.
>
> > Whoopee ti yi yo, git along little dogies,
> > It's your misfortune, and none of my own.
> > Whoopee ti yi yo, git along little dogies,
> > For you know Wyoming will be your new home.[7]

In 1947, just a year before his death at the age of eighty, John Lomax's autobiography, *Adventures of a Ballad Hunter*, was published by Macmillan. In chapter 3 the great collector told about his introduction to "Whoopee Ti Yi Yo": it was not a cowboy but a woman—a guitar-strumming gypsy fortune-teller in Fort Worth—who first sang it for him. When she had finished she had this to say: "To me

... that's the loveliest of all cowboy songs. Like others, its rhythm comes from the movement of a horse. It is not the roisterous, hell-for-leather, wild gallop of 'The Old Chisholm Trail,' nor the easy canter of 'Goodbye, Old Paint.' You mustn't frighten the dogies.... Lope around them gently in the darkness as you sing about punching them along to their new home in Wyoming. They'll sleep the night through and never have a bad dream."[8]

When Owen Wister, who was a trained musician, first heard the song in 1893, he, too, took down the air as well as the words. Apparently this also remained hidden in his desk, until 1932, when he presented the music to John Lomax, who incorporated it into *American Ballads and Folk Songs*, first published in 1934 by Macmillan. It can be found in the current printing, along with a page of comments on the song by the author of *The Virginian*.[9]

With the advent of radio broadcasting in the 1920s, "Whoopee Ti Yi Yo," together with the best of the other old-time cowboy songs, enjoyed wide popularity. It, of course, has been put on records (dozens of them), has been issued in sheet music (presumably for the use of concert singers), and over the years has appeared in numberless printed song collections. In 1927 Carl Sandburg included it in his memorable and durable volume *The American Songbag*, with the following note: "This widely sung piece ... has the smell of saddle leather and long reaches of level prairies in it. It is plainly of Irish origin, connecting with the lilts and the ballads that begin, 'As I was a-walking one morning.' "[10]

In recent years several authorities on the subject have stated that the unknown composer of "Whoopee Ti Yi Yo" modeled his song on an old Irish ballad about an old man rocking a cradle which had these lines:

> As I was a-walking one evening for pleasure,
> Down by the still waters I joggled along,
> I met an old man making sad lamentation,
> And nursing a baby that's none of his own.
> Ee-ay-oh, my laddie, lie easy,
> It's my misfortune and none of your own,
> That she leaves me here weeping and rocking the cradle,
> Minding a baby that's none of my own.[11]

The second stanza of Owen Wister's version of "Whoopee Ti Yi Yo" begins with this descriptive bit:

> In the Springtime we round up the dogies,
> Slap on the brands and bob off their tails.

Following an ancient custom introduced into America by the early Spaniards, the ranch hands in this old drawing are burning the owner's trademark into the hide of an apprehensive calf. Brands ran all the way from the cattleman's initials to objects as varied as rocking chairs, broken hearts, spectacles, frying pans, and pitchforks. An experienced stockman always sought a brand that could not be easily altered. The illustration is from *New Colorado and the Santa Fe Trail* by A. A. Hayes, Jr., published in 1880 by Harper & Brothers.

The unknown composer of these lines managed to condense into one short sentence several lengthy pages from the early history of North America's cattle industry. For a more revealing and exciting prose description of the frantic preparations for a trail drive north out of the Lone Star State nearly a century ago, we are indebted to two veteran western authors, Will Croft Barnes and William McLeod Raine. The following word-portrait of this extremely complex operation is from their book *Cattle*, published by Doubleday in 1930 and reissued in 1936 by Grosset & Dunlap as *Cattle, Cowboys and Rangers*.

In putting up a trail herd Cattleland was at its busiest. If the gather began the middle of February, it was likely to be the end of the first week in March before the stock was out of the thicket, cut, road-branded, and inspected. The last days before the drive started were, if possible, more hectic than those when four-year-olds were being harried out of the prickly pear.

Heat and dust . . . Dust and heat . . . Perspiration pouring down the grimy faces of vaqueros, sweat dried on the roan flanks of mustangs . . . Bawling of uneasy cows, blatting of frightened calves dragged out of the herd to the fire . . . A flanker in striped trousers "going down the rope," and throwing the flitter-ear by an upward and outward pressure of the knees against the side . . . The sizzle of the red hot iron on the hide of a maverick, stretched taut . . . Shouts of lank brown youths on the swing after bolting dogies . . . Raucous curse and gay banter . . . Rounding up of the remuda, breaking of outlaw mustangs, choosing of mounts, all geldings, solid colors preferred, combing of burrs out of tangled manes and forelocks . . . Overhauling of saddle and bridle, mending of broken wagons . . . Moulding bullets, cleaning of guns . . . Checking up on supplies—cheap coffee, salt sidemeat, meal, flour, saleratus, sorghum.

From long before daylight until deep into the night all hands on the jump . . . Through the starlit hours of darkness riders circling the sleeping herd and singing lullabies, gospel hymns, or ribald range songs . . . "Hold the fort, for I am coming," the apologia of one herder lifting into the velvety night, and

> I'm wild and wooly and full of fleas,
> Never been curried below the knees,
> I'm an ole she-wolf from Bitter Creek,
> An' it's my main night to h-o-w-l—

the careless response of another.[12]

Folksingers and even today's western cowboys might well be puzzled by the second half of the line in "Whoopee Ti Yi Yo" reading "Slap on the brands and bob off their tails." This appears to be exactly what happened to many a beef critter tapped to take the long walk up the Chisholm Trail from Texas to a railhead in Kansas. Shortening tails, along with applying a "road brand," made quick identification easy in case the herd stampeded and got mixed up with local cattle along the way. The animals comprising a large trail herd might carry the brands of half a dozen original owners.

In *Up the Trail in '79*, one of the few eyewitness accounts of an early cattle drive, the author, a Texan named Baylis John Fletcher, describes the final steps—one might say the final indignities—in the process of preparing the dogies for the arduous overland trip.

We had collected about two thousand cattle and were ready to hit the trail. Before starting our long journey, however, we must road-brand our cattle. Our road brand was T-L connected. To burn these letters on the sides of two thousand cattle, we must first drive them into a customary chute, or narrow lane, just wide enough for one cow to squeeze through and long enough to hold twenty-five animals. After we had branded the imprisoned animals by poking a red hot branding iron through the fence of the chute, we cropped their tails as an additional mark to indicate that they were trail cattle.[13]

Owen Wister's 1893 Texas diary also contains some interesting sidelights on the subject of trail driving together with an observation on the old-time cowpuncher's habit of singing while on night guard.

The personnel needed to control while driving, say 3,300 head, after the cattle have been broken in to traveling on the plains is the cook with eight men around the herd. One of these is the boss, or foreman, who receives $100 a month where the others receive from $35 to $40. The boss takes his turn night herding and is not unlike the captain of a ship, ready to turn in everywhere on an emergency. There is also sometimes a second boss, whose position is one of difficulty on account of jealousy. His pay is about $45, or was from '83 on. Sometimes there is an extra man to herd the horses ridden by the other men. He rides in the wagon in the day time with the cook, who drives, and at night he herds the horses. This is unusual, however. Commonly the men take turns looking after the horses by day and at night hobble them. Each man has usually four horses, which form his "string.". . .

. . .In delivering a bunch of 100 or 50 to the trail herd before it starts, it is not essential (as later when trailing has begun) to let the animals lie down at night. Pens are used, and inside these the men on guard ride among the cattle and prod them or otherwise keep them on their feet. This is because, being on their feet, they make a continual movement and disturbance among each other; whereas when all are bedded down and utterly quiet, the starting up of a rabbit, the passing of a dog, or the striking of a match will be very likely to startle them and stampede them at once. Singing to quiet the cattle is important. The more restless they are, the louder or more inarticulate is the singing, no words being used at all, but only a strange wailing. But as the cattle grow quiet, the music gathers form, and while the herd lies quietly at rest on the plain, the night herders are apt to sing long definite songs as they ride round and round the edges.[14]

NOTES

An earlier version of this chapter appeared under the title "Owen Wister and the Dogies" in the *Journal of American Folklore*, 82 (Jan.-Mar., 1969), 66–69.

1. John White and George Shackley, *The Lonesome Cowboy: Songs of the Plains and Hills*

(New York: Al Piantadosi, 1929), pp. 8–10. This folio is currently available from music publisher Jerry Vogel, 121 West 45th Street, New York, New York 10036.

2. "Git Along Little Dogies" is one of three songs of the Old West discussed in the revised and enlarged edition of *The Book of World-Famous Music: Classical, Popular and Folk* by James J. Fuld (New York: Crown Publishers, 1971). The others included in his list of nearly a thousand songs are "Home on the Range," the subject of chapter 14 in my own book, and "Oh, Bury Me Not on the Lone Prairie," whose interesting history is documented in detail by Fuld.

3. Fanny Kemble Wister, *Owen Wister Out West: His Journals and Letters* (Chicago: University of Chicago Press, 1958), pp. 153–54.

4. Andy Adams, *The Log of a Cowboy* (Boston and New York: Houghton Mifflin Co., 1903), p. 313.

5. For more on the word *dogie* see p. 95.

6. Sharlot M. Hall, "Old Range Days and New in Arizona," *Out West*, Mar., 1908, p.181.

7. John A. Lomax, *Cowboy Songs and Other Frontier Ballads* (New York: Sturgis & Walton Co., 1910), pp. 87, 88.

8. John A. Lomax, *Adventures of a Ballad Hunter* (New York: Macmillan Co., 1947), pp. 44–45.

9. John A. Lomax and Alan Lomax, *American Ballads and Folk Songs* (New York: Macmillan Co., 1934), pp. 386–87, 389.

10. Carl Sandburg, *The American Songbag* (New York: Harcourt, Brace and Co., 1927), pp. 268–70.

11. Oscar Brand, *The Ballad Mongers* (New York: Funk & Wagnalls, 1962), pp. 44–45. See also Alan Lomax, *The Folk Songs of North America* (Garden City, N.Y.: Doubleday and Co., 1960), p. 375, and Irwin Silber and Earl Robinson, *Songs of the Great American West* (New York: Macmillan Co., 1967), p. 173.

12. Will Croft Barnes and William McLeod Raine, *Cattle* (New York: Doubleday and Co., 1930), pp. 75–76.

13. Baylis John Fletcher, *Up the Trail in '79* (Norman: University of Oklahoma Press, 1968), pp. 14–15.

14. Wister, *Owen Wister Out West*, pp. 159, 161.

2

Owen Wister, Songwriter

Philadelphian Owen Wister (1860–1938) authored more than twenty books and, although it is virtually forgotten today, placed his brand on a handful of musical compositions.[1] Only one of the books, *The Virginian*, that world-famous tale of cowboy life in Wyoming of the 1880s and Wister's sole western novel, has remained in print continuously ever since it topped the fiction best seller list of 1902. Wister's one song with a western setting—"Ten Thousand Cattle Straying"—disappeared from the music store counters long ago. Even so, there was something about it that people remembered. As a result, it is still a favorite with dude ranch entertainers and other singers in that region Wister liked to call "cattle land." And every so often during the past forty-odd years a variant has turned up in a printed collection whose compiler apparently had no knowledge of the song's ultimate source.[2]

Even ballad hunter John A. Lomax, although acquainted with Wister, failed to associate the author of *The Virginian* with a song titled "Ten Thousand Cattle" when, in 1938, he included it in the revised and enlarged edition of *Cowboys Songs and Other Frontier Ballads*. A footnote simply stated that Lomax had taken it from Margaret Larkin's anthology *Singing Cowboy*, published in 1931 by Alfred A. Knopf.

During the 1930s half a dozen cowboy song folios issued by firms in New York's Tin Pan Alley carried variants of the song without credit to anyone, as did that handsome, lavishly illustrated 1965 publication *Songs of Man*, compiled by Norman Luboff and Win Stracke and issued by Prentice-Hall and the Walton Music Corporation.

Music had been Wister's first love. He studied it at Harvard, hoping to become a composer, and after graduation spent a winter at the

In this picture of Owen Wister supplied by his daughter, Mrs. Walter Stokes, the future famous writer of western fiction appears not to have yet "learned the ropes." The snapshot probably was taken on one of his earliest visits to Wyoming.

Paris Conservatory. Writing also had been one of his chief interests while in college. However, faced with making a living, he opted for the law as a profession. But after five summers spent in Wyoming he turned his back on the bar and became a full-time writer of western fiction. His first published western story, "Hank's Woman," appeared in *Harper's Weekly Magazine* for August 27, 1892. Ten years later his only novel of the West, *The Virginian*, went to the top of the best seller list at home and was soon being translated into numerous foreign languages.

Considering the success of the book both at home and abroad and the fact that the author's grandmother was the well-known English actress Fanny Kemble, it was only natural that Wister should try dramatizing the adventures of his popular cowboy hero whose punch line—"When you call me that, *smile!*"—was earning his creator a ticket of admission to the pages of *Bartlett's Familiar Quotations*. In collaboration with Kirke La Shelle, a prominent author-producer, Wister fashioned a play, also called *The Virginian*, with Dustin Farnum in the title role and a cast of twenty-eight characters. Opening in New York on

"'When you call me that, smile.'"

A saloon in Medicine Bow, Wyoming, setting for the most famous line Owen Wister ever wrote, as pictured by artist Arthur I. Keller for the first edition of *The Virginian* (1902).

January 5, 1904, this had a fair run on Broadway and was on the road for many years, first with Farnum in the lead role, later with William S. Hart, prior to the latter's entry into films. As late as 1937 it was being presented in summer stock. The *New York Times* for August 10 of that year described a production at Mount Kisco, New York, with Henry Fonda as the hero.

Possibly to lighten up the rather heavy stage proceedings, which include a hanging and two shootings, Wister composed "Ten Thousand Cattle Straying" for Frank Campeau, who played the villain Trampas and, as in the novel, eventually received his comeuppance from the hand of the Virginian. The song served as a trademark for Trampas on stage and when heard sung in the wings alerted the audience to the lying, thieving polecat's presence. Witmark & Sons published it in sheet music in 1904, with photographs of cowpokes Farnum and Campeau decorating the front cover.

In his book *Stirrup High*, which describes his childhood in Montana, that prolific writer of western stories, Walt Coburn, tells of having witnessed a performance of *The Virginian*.

> After dinner at a hotel with father and my brothers, I walked down the street feeling warm and good inside. I didn't know a kid in town my age so I was going on a high lonesome. I had money in my pocket and there was nothing to stop me from painting the town a strawberry-pop red. As I walked along whistling through my teeth I kept thinking of the play I had seen at the Great Falls Opera House—Dustin Farnum in *The Virginian*. I remembered the song Trampas sang and I started humming it as I headed across the tracks for Doc Murray's Drug Store for a soda pop and some ice cream and candy.

> > Ten thousand cattle straying. . .
> > I quit my range and traveled away.
> > So it's sons a guns,
> > That's what I say!
> > I've gambled my money
> > All away![3]

Back in 1934 I published a pamphlet containing songs and poems by Montana cowboy D. J. O'Malley. This I mailed to prominent folklorists and others with a special interest in cowboys and the West, among them Owen Wister, whose address I had found in a footnote in the Lomax volume *American Ballads and Folk Songs*, which came out that year. As the famous author had not heard about the new Lomax book, one letter led to another, and a few months later I was writing Owen Wister concerning the history of "Ten Thousand Cattle Straying." I said I had seen it in Margaret Larkin's book *Singing Cowboy*,

TEN THOUSAND CATTLE STRAYING
(DEAD BROKE)

DUSTIN FARNUM AS "THE VIRGINIAN"

SUNG AS AN
INCIDENTAL FEATURE
IN
KIRKE LA SHELLE'S
PRODUCTION

THE VIRGINIAN

MR FRANK CAMPEAU AS TRAMPAS

WORDS & MUSIC BY
OWEN WISTER

M. WITMARK & SONS
NEW YORK CHICAGO LONDON SAN FRANCISCO
JOSEF WEINBERGER LEIPZIG AND VIENNA
ALLAN & CO MELBOURNE AUSTRALIA
CANADIAN AMERICAN MUSIC CO LTD TORONTO

50¢
2/- NET.

31

Ten Thousand Cattle Straying.

(DEAD BROKE.)

Words and Music by OWEN WISTER.

Ten __ thous - and cat - tle __ stray - ing, They __
My __ girl she has went __ stray - ing, She __
So __ I've took to card play - ing, I __
My __ luck has all gone __ stray - ing, I __

6213-3

quit   my   range   and   trav - ell'd a - way,   And it's
quit   me   too   and   trav - ell'd a - way,   With a
deal   the   decks   but it   don't   seem to pay,   And it's
make   no   strike   by   night   or   day,   But it's

"sons - of guns" is   what I say,   I am dead broke, dead
"son - of - a - gun" from I - o - way,   I'm a lone man, lone
"son - of - a - gun-ner" I get each day, And noth - ing will come, will
"sons - of - guns" I still will say, For I'm in the game, the

broke this day.
man this day.
come my way.
game to stay.   **CHORUS.** *(half spoken.)*

In gam - bling hells de -

Dead broke.

6243 - 3

33

Git Along, Little Dogies

with no clue to its origin, although someone had told me that he had composed it. A facsimile of his reply appears here. He apparently felt flattered, rather than resentful, that his work had been handed about from singer to singer over the years and had eventually been put into printed song collections as a traditional western whose composer was unknown.

Wister's special interest in music is reflected in his habit of having characters in a number of his western stories render snatches of song. In chapter 9 of *The Virginian* (1902), the hero sings the following, which the author states is the only printable stanza out of seventy-nine.

> If you go to monkey with my Looloo girl,
> I'll tell you what I'll do:
> I'll cyarve your heart with my razor, AND
> I'll shoot you with my pistol, too—[4]

Chapter 14 of *The Virginian* describes a group rendition of a familiar oldie from cattle land.

> I'm wild, and woolly, and full of fleas;
> I'm hard to curry above the knees;
> I'm a she-wolf from Bitter Creek, and
> It's my night to ho-o-wl—[5]

Wister's yarn "The Jimmyjohn Boss," which led off his short story collection by the same name published in 1900, has three drunken Idaho cowboys each contribute a stanza of the following. The author refers to it as "an old coast song."

> Once, jes' onced in the year o' '49,
> I met a fancy thing by the name o' Keroline;
> I never could persuade her for to leave me be;
> She went and she took and she married me.
>
> Once, once again in the year o' '64,
> By the city of Whatcom down along the shore—
> I never could persuade them for to leave me be—
> A Siwash squaw went and took and married me.
>
> Once, once again in the year o' '71
> ('Twas the suddenest deed that I ever done)—
> I never could persuade them for to leave me be—
> A rich banker's daughter she took and married me.[6]

Lin McLean, a collection of Wister short stories with the same Wyoming cowboy as the central figure throughout, was issued in 1898. The book ends on a dismal note—the burial of a dance hall girl

807, REAL ESTATE TRUST BUILDING
PHILADELPHIA

Philadelphia, November 28, 1934.

John White, Esq.,
Canterbury Road,
Westfield, N.J.

Dear Mr. White:-

Yes, I can tell you exactly about that song "Ten Thousand Cattle".

After several visits to Wyoming, I wrote it in camp there, in the summer of 1888. No song resembling it, in the least, that I ever heard, existed at that time. I set it from the air of an old French opera. Six years afterwards, when it came to producing a dramatization of my book "The Virginian", it struck me that the song would make a good point in the play, if used in the way of what is now called a theme song. I did not want to use the tune of the French opera and I composed one of my own. When "The Virginian" was produced, which I think was in the autumn of 1903, with Dustin Farnum in the title rôle and Frank Campau in the rôle of Trampas, I taught the song to Frank Campau, who sang it at various points in the play. It was published by Witmark about that time. The fact that it was published in a collection of cowpunchers songs in a version which bore only very faint traces of the original, is a very pretty demonstration of the way many a popular ballad was gradually developed.

I hope this is what you want.

Yours very truly,

Owen Wister

Assuming Wister's statement about writing "Ten Thousand Cattle Straying" in 1888 is correct, he erred in saying "six years afterwards." He meant "sixteen," because the stage version of *The Virginian* opened at New York in January, 1904.

by a group of cowboys well fortified with firewater. The mourners see nothing incongruous in closing the ceremony with the singing of a stanza and chorus of what they refer to as "The Lament."

> Once in the saddle I used to go dashing,
> Once in the saddle I used to go gay;
> First took to drinking, and then to card-playing;
> Got shot in the body, and now here I lay.

> Beat the drum slowly,
> Play the fife lowly,
> Sound the dead march as you bear me along.
> Take me to Boot-hill, and throw the sod over me—
> I'm but a poor cow-boy, I know I done wrong.[7]

NOTES

An earlier version of this chapter appeared in *Western Folklore*, 26 (Oct., 1967), 269–71.

1. Disparate examples are "Kiss Me, Clairette, Suzette, Yvette," with words and music by Owen Wister, published by G. Schirmer (New York) in 1919, and three Shakespeare songs with piano arrangements by Wister—"Sigh No More, Ladies," "Winter's Song," and "Amiens Sings"— issued by Schirmer in 1936, just two years before Wister's death at the age of seventy-eight.

2. An exception is Glenn Ohrlin, *The Hell-Bound Train: A Cowboy Songbook* (Urbana: University of Illinois Press, 1973), pp. 15, 248–49.

3. Walt Coburn, *Stirrup High* (New York: Julian Messner, 1957), p. 77.

4. Owen Wister, *The Virginian* (New York and London: Macmillan Co., 1902), p. 96.

5. Ibid., p. 162. This is essentially the opening stanza of a six-stanza poem, "The Drunken Desperado," printed in the 1919 John A. Lomax anthology *Songs of the Cattle Trail and Cow Camp* (New York: Macmillan Co.), pp. 44–45, and credited to Baird Boyd. Cf. above, p. 24.

6. Owen Wister, *The Jimmyjohn Boss* (New York and London: Harper & Brothers Publishers, 1900), p. 43.

7. Owen Wister, *Lin McLean* (New York and London: Harper & Brothers Publishers, 1898), p. 274. Wister appears to have been the first to put these famous lines between the covers of a book. Ten years later, N. Howard Thorp included six stanzas and a chorus in his pioneer anthology *Songs of the Cowboys* (Estancia, N.Mex.: News Print Shop, 1908), pp. 29–30, using the title "Cow Boys Lament." In their book reviewing Thorp's work, *Songs of the Cowboys, by N. Howard ("Jack") Thorp* (New York: Clarkson N. Potter, Bramhall House, 1966), Austin and Alta Fife describe "The Cowboy's Lament" as "the most famous of all cowboy songs" (p. 148) and devote forty-three pages to its long and colorful history.

3

Last Day with the Longhorns

That history can be written in verse as well as in prose is evident from the following stanzas composed by Joseph Mills Hanson of Yankton, South Dakota, first printed in *Leslie's Monthly Magazine* for October, 1904, and destined to become a famous song typifying the American cowboy.

We are up in the morning ere dawning of day
And the grub wagon's busy and flap-jacks[1] in play;
While the herd is astir over hillside and swale[2]
With the night-riders rounding them into the trail.

Come, take up your cinchas[3]
And shake up your reins;
Come, wake up your bronco
And break for the plains;
Come, roust those red steers from the long chaparral,[4]
For the outfit is off for the railroad corral!

The sun circles upward, the steers as they plod
Are pounding to powder the hot prairie sod
And, it seems, as the dust turns you dizzy and sick
That you'll never reach noon and the cool, shady creek.

But tie up your kerchief[5]
And ply up your nag;
Come, dry up your grumbles
And try not to lag;
Come, larrup[6] those steers from the long chaparral,
For we're far on the way to the railroad corral!

The afternoon shadows are starting to lean
When the grub wagon sticks in a marshy ravine
And the herd scatters further than vision can look,
For you bet all true punchers will help out the cook!

> So shake out your rawhide[7]
> And snake it up fair;
> Come, break your old bronco
> To taking his share!
> Come, now for the steers in the long chaparral,
> For it's all in the drive to the railroad corral!

But the longest of days must reach evening at last,
When the hills are all climbed and the creeks are all passed
And the tired herd droops in the yellowing light;
Let them loaf if they will, for the railroad's in sight!

> So flap up your holster
> And snap up your belt;
> Come, strap up the saddle
> Whose lap you have felt;
> Good-by to the steers and the long chaparral!
> There's a town that's a trump[8] by the railroad corral![9]

Here is a true-to-life western portrait, its subject a saddle-weary trail crew pushing a herd of Longhorn beef steers along the seemingly endless prairie amid the dust and heat of summer. For days, perhaps for weeks, these hard-working cowpunchers have faced up to the hazards of their unique occupation—fording creeks, swimming rivers, meeting the dangers inherent in midnight stampedes caused by a sudden clap of thunder or the hooting of an owl, outwitting cow thieves and marauding Indians, and pausing every so often to haul the indispensable chuck wagon out of the mud.

Undoubtedly the men had plenty to grumble about as the long line of cattle plodded along, covering only about a dozen miles a day. Their sentiments possibly were best expressed in these lines from one of the oldest American cowboy songs, "The Old Chisholm Trail," as I like to sing them:

> It's bacon and beans most every day;
> I'd as soon be eating prairie hay.
>
> No chaps, no slicker, and it's pourin' down rain,
> I swear, by God, I'll never night-herd again.
>
> I'll sell my outfit as fast as I can,
> And I won't punch cows for no damn man.

But now there is a feeling of relief as a little town with its cattle

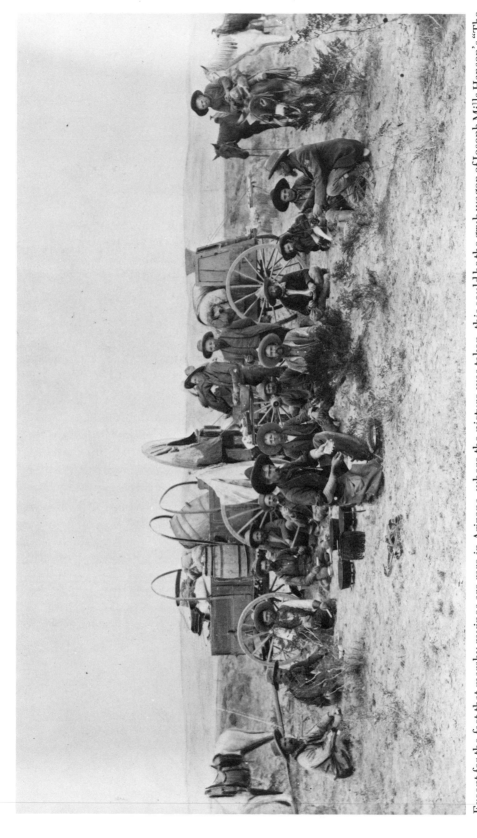

Except for the fact that marshy ravines are rare in Arizona, where the picture was taken, this could be the grub wagon of Joseph Mills Hanson's "The Railroad Corral," now safely out of the mud and back in the business of feeding hungry cowhands. The photograph was supplied by the Arizona Historical Society at Tucson, with the following caption: "Chow time at the C O Bar round-up near Mesa Butte on the Cedar Ranch spread, 1907."

pens beside the railroad tracks shows up on the horizon. By dusk the tired, sweaty riders will say good-bye and good riddance to those cantankerous dogies soon to be aboard cattle cars for the final leg of the long journey from the ranch to beef-hungry cities of the East. Tonight there is celebrating to be done. Tomorrow? No doubt a big headache. The day after tomorrow? A haircut and, provided the wages haven't all been gambled away, some new clothes before saddling up again for the long ride back home.

The scene described so aptly by Hanson recalls the great trail-driving period in the Southwest that began shortly after the Civil War and continued for more than two decades. The close of the war found the vast cattle-breeding regions of Texas overstocked with the famed Longhorns but short on satisfactory ways of getting the meat crop to market. Old trails to eastern Kansas and Missouri used by drovers prior to 1861 were closing down as the area filled up with farmers. A happy solution to the problem came when, in the summer of 1867, a far-sighted twenty-nine-year-old Illinois cattle dealer named Joseph G. McCoy began building corrals and a siding at Abilene, Kansas, on the new Kansas Pacific Railroad.

The youthful entrepreneur advertised widely in Texas. Before his stockyard was completed, mile-long herds of from two to three thousand rangy steers were strung out along the Chisholm Trail, some prodded along by horsemen still wearing tattered Confederate uniforms, and all heading for the little prairie town of Abilene, then consisting of fewer than two dozen log houses and stores plus a six-room hotel. On September 5, 1867, a locomotive's whistle signaled the beginning of an era as the first trainload of live beef, twenty cars long, chugged off McCoy's siding headed for Chicago.

Although Abilene prospered from its new business, after five years the neighboring farmers grew tired of having their fences and crops trampled, and the town fathers were fed up with the vice and gunplay attendant on the annual influx of wild cowboys from Texas. Accordingly, in 1872 the trail drivers were advised officially to go elsewhere. Wichita and Ellsworth were quick to take advantage of Abilene's abdication and of the bonanza created by what was now a veritable flood of cattle moving northward from Texas every summer. The riches and notoriety also were shared by Newton and Caldwell, later by the greatest and wickedest cow town of them all, Dodge City.

During the 1880s many large herds of young Texas-born stock also were driven north as far as Wyoming and Montana for fattening on the lush pastures there before being shipped to market. This helped Miles City, Montana, earn a reputation as a wild cow town second only to that

This fanciful drawing of a cattle car about to be converted into kio kindling as too many wild Longhorns are forced into it appeared in *Frank Leslie's Illustrated Newspaper* for August 19, 1871. The setting is the railroad corral at Abilene, Kansas, first railhead to receive live Texas beef driven north over the storied Chisholm Trail. According to Will C. Barnes ("The Vanishing Longhorns," *Saturday Evening Post*, October 15, 1927), five dollars a head for huge four- and five-year-old steers was the price paid at the railroad shipping point for the first herds to reach Kansas. But at the time this seemed like real money to hard-up, over-stocked Texas ranchers. Later, Barnes said, prices rose to fifteen and twenty dollars.

held by Dodge. By the end of the 1880s the number of Texas trail herds was dwindling rapidly as barbed wire fences and farming homesteaders blocked off the routes and concurrently the railroads began serving west Texas directly.

Joseph Mills Hanson's poetic description of the final day of a trail drive has had a curious history. Back in 1933 he told me that when he sent it to *Leslie's* he titled it "Cowboy Song" and stated he had written it to fit the air of the well-known Scottish ballad "Bonnie Dundee." [10] The editor either lost or disregarded this footnote. In spite of this, the verses somehow acquired a tune and soon were in circulation as a western folksong, with the title "The Railroad Corral." Over the years they have been printed in numerous songbooks and included on phonograph records. Editors of elementary school music books recently have begun including "The Railroad Corral" among their selections with an authentic western flavor. But its author received not one bit of recognition from songbook editors until 1968, when Richard

"It's hooping and yelling and cursing those dogies" as a rampaging herd of Texas Longhorns bound for Dodge City, Kansas, takes over the main street of a prairie town in this drawing from *Frank Leslie's Illustrated Newspaper* for July 27, 1878. The cowboys are attempting to control the cattle with cow whips made of closely braided rawhide. Sometimes as long as twenty feet, these were also a formidable weapon. An expert could snap off a rattlesnake's head with a flick of the wrist. Not all trail bosses permitted the use of whips.

E. Lingenfelter and Richard A. Dwyer issued their monumental volume *Songs of the American West* (University of California Press), which gives the origin of "The Railroad Corral." When this colorful word-picture of a day on the cow trail was first turned into a song it became a maverick, and to the day Hanson died, in 1960 at the age of eighty-four, he never succeeded in putting his brand back on it. There is more than a touch of irony in the fact that while he wrote five books on the history of the West, the best known being *Conquest of the Missouri*, first published in 1909, all of them together never came to the attention of as many readers as did this one poem which is still circulating widely as an anonymous contribution to native American musical literature.

While most printed versions of "The Railroad Corral" are quite faithful to the original, an unusual departure appears in a sixth-grade songbook, *This Is Music*, Book 6, issued in 1962 by Allyn and Bacon. Using the age-old prerogative of the folksinger, one of the editors, Robert E. Nye, a professor at the University of Oregon, contributed two new stanzas of his own. These deal with a cattle drive from the

Joseph Mills Hanson photographed in 1937. Born at Yankton, South Dakota, in 1876, he served with his native state's National Guard on the Mexican border in 1916 and in World War I became chief of the Historic Section of the General Staff. Hanson contributed poems and articles to the AEF newspaper, *Stars & Stripes,* later wrote and lectured widely on the conflict. In 1934 he joined the National Park Service at Jamestown, Virginia, as a historian; from 1942 through 1947 he was superintendent of Manassas Battlefield National Park. Manassas, Virginia, remained his home until his death.

historic Pete French Ranch in the Blitzen Valley at Frenchglen, Oregon, to the Union Pacific Railroad at Winnemucca, Nevada, at one time an important shipping center for cattle and sheep.

> Steens Mountain is east and we're well on our way;
> We'll drive south to Blitzen and stop at midday.
> The heat of the sun is upon us at noon,
> And the herd will be glad at the rise of the moon.
>
> For days we have traveled the dry, barren land;
> Sometimes we grow weary of dust and of sand.
> Just over the hill from the last chaparral, is
> Winnemucca, Nevada, and the railroad corral.[11]

NOTES

An earlier version of this chapter appeared under the title "Curious History of 'The Railroad Corral' " in *Southwest Heritage*, 4 (Dec., 1969), 11–13.

1. *Flap-jacks*—large pancakes.
2. *Swale*—a hollow or depression, especially in wet, marshy ground.
3. *Cinchas*—saddle girths; short bands of coarsely woven horsehair or canvas that go under the horse's belly to keep the saddle in place.
4. *Chaparral*—a dense thicket.
5. *Kerchief*—the cowboy's bandanna neckerchief that could be pulled up over the nose and mouth to keep out the dust.
6. *Larrup*—beat or whip. In this case it means about the same as *roust* in the first stanza—rout or drive out.
7. *Rawhide*—a lasso made of thin strips of braided rawhide (cowskin).
8. *Trump*—The poet apparently intended this in the card-playing sense. To a trail crew that had been on the prairie for weeks, a little railroad town with its dance hall and stores looked better than anything they had seen in a long while.
9. *Leslie's Monthly Magazine*, 58 (Oct., 1904), 681.
10. Hanson had made a similar statement concerning "Bonnie Dundee" in a letter printed in the *Literary Digest* for April 25, 1914, p. 985. In reviewing the first Lomax anthology the *Digest* had referred to "The Railroad Corral" and other cowboy songs as "the palpable result of group improvisation" (Feb. 21, 1914, pp. 379–80), whereupon poet Hanson took pen in hand to set the record straight.
11. William R. Sur et al., *This Is Music*, Book 6 (Boston: Allyn and Bacon, 1962), p. 23.

4

Singin' to 'em

One sure way of getting a modern cowpoke to ask "Are you kidding?" would be to tell him that the old-time puncher of eighty or ninety years ago had a habit of singing to the cows, particularly when night-herding on the trail or during a roundup. Should said modern cowpoke through some miracle have access to the article "Banjo in the Cow Camps," written thirty-odd years ago by New Mexico troubadour and ballad collector N. Howard "Jack" Thorp, he could prove you wrong by quoting Thorp, who wrote as follows:

> It is generally thought that cowboys did a lot of singing around the herd at night to quiet them on the bed ground. I have been asked about this, and I'll say that I have stood my share of night watches in fifty years and I seldom heard any singing of that kind. What you would hear as you passed your partner on guard would be a kind of low hum or whistle, and you wouldn't know what it was. Just some old hymn tune, like as not—something to kill time and not bad enough to make the herd want to get up and run.[1]

Thorp's comment on this intriguing subject appears to be very much of a minority report. Among the eye- or rather ear-witnesses who are on record as agreeing that singing to cattle at night once was standard operating procedure are Arizona's cowboy-author Will Croft Barnes, Montana cowboys "Teddy Blue" Abbott and D. J. O'Malley, diarist Owen Wister, rancher-poet Badger Clark, and pioneer ballad hunter John Avery Lomax. Numerous able historians are also in this camp, among them J. Frank Dobie, Emerson Hough, Walter Prescott Webb, Wayne Gard, and Ramon Adams.[2]

In his book *The Old-Time Cowhand*, Adams says, "The practice [of singing to cattle on bed ground] got to be so common that night herdin' was spoken of as 'singin' to 'em.' "[3] In *The Longhorns*, Dobie states: "Singing, whistling, chanting, humming seemed to have a soothing effect on the toughest old Longhorns. Most of all, the sounds—supposed to be harmonious—prevented any sudden noise from startling the cattle. 'It was cloudy in the west and a-lookin' like rain'—and the boss would say, 'Boys, I reckon you'll have to sing to 'em tonight.' "[4]

We are told that there was considerable vocalizing daytimes, too, as herds of Longhorns plodded up dusty cattle trails from Texas to railway shipping points in Kansas or to pastures in Montana and Wyoming. John Lomax refers to this daytime singing in his autobiography.[5] J. Frank Dobie, Texas folklorist extraordinary, when writing in the weekly *Country Gentleman* for January 10, 1925, penned this colorful word-picture of a typical trail crew indulging in song at every opportunity. Some readers will no doubt feel that Dobie's statement about cowboys singing for the pleasure of the cattle needs to be taken with a tiny grain of salt.

> Imagine a late afternoon in advancing spring fifty years ago [ca. 1875]. Somewhere between Brownsville and the head waters of the Missouri a herd of stock cattle is strung out for a mile. I say "stock cattle," for cows and calves and young stuff need a hundred times more nursing and watching over than beef cattle.
>
> The leaders of the herd are walking out as though they scented water and bed-ground grazing. On either side of the lead cattle, riding slowly and carelessly, are the point men. Strung out at long intervals behind them come the swing men. Often one of these stops to let his horse catch a mouthful of grass; now and then one pushes sharply ahead or rides toward the rear to shove in an animal that is picking its way too far out.
>
> At the rear, or drag, of the herd come the drag men. Their job is not easy, for they have to keep constantly after a few lagging crowbait cows, played-out calves, and sore-footed yearlings.
>
> The men are not hurried. They ride too far apart to talk to one another. Now and then they yell at the cattle. They pop whips—unless the boss is one of those cowmen that don't allow whips.
>
> They sing.
>
> The day, the herd, the outfit I have been picturing was like hundreds of other days, herds, outfits of the trail days. It is a picture of fact, not fancy.
>
> Of course not all the cowboys on all days sang. Many a waddie could no more carry a tune than he could carry a buffalo bull. Often all hands were too busy fighting and "cussin' them dad-blamed cattle" to sing. But in general the cowboys sang.

J. Frank Dobie (1888–1964), prolific writer on the Southwest and a prime mover in the Texas Folk-Lore Society. Photograph from the University Writings Collections, Austin, Texas.

They sang sometimes for the pure joy of singing—for their own pleasure. Again they sang to the cattle—for the pleasure of the cattle.

They sang of cows and of life in the cow country, of round-ups, stampedes, prairie dogs, rattlesnakes, chuck wagons, ropes, spurs, and bad horses.

They sang also of bad men, Indian fights, squatters, buffalo hunters, mule skinners, prospectors and Tom Sherman's saloon in Dodge City, the cowboy capital—of the whole frontier of which they were a part.

They sang of the mothers and homes and sweethearts that softened their memories.

"Git along, my little dogies," and the herds snailed their way on, westward and northward, across an empire of range land on which there was neither fence nor furrow. It was a lonely vastness.

Cattle are not so sensitive as horses, but like horses and men they crave companionship, and the herds seemed to steady and to travel better by the sound of song.

It was at night, though, when the cattle were restless and likely to stampede, that singing was a necessity. Then every puncher had a chance to sing out all the verses of all the songs he could recollect and a still better chance to invent and practice new ones.[6]

Dobie's close friend, historian Walter Prescott Webb, in his landmark volume *The Great Plains*, offers this comment: "Men have always sung at their work, especially those who have worked much alone; but the cowboy found singing a part of his occupation, a necessary accomplishment of his trade. The singing soothed the cattle and distracted their attention from sudden noises that might have caused them to stampede, and who knows but it comforted them in other ways?"[7]

Picturesque "Teddy Blue" Abbott, whose frank recollections of an exciting cowpunching career begun in the 1870s have become a classic, made numerous references to singing to cattle. This one is from chapter 24 of his famous autobiography, *We Pointed Them North*:

One reason I believe there was so many songs about cowboys was the custom we had of singing to the cattle on night herd. The singing was supposed to soothe them and it did; I don't know why, unless it was that a sound they was used to would keep them from spooking at other noises. . . . The two men on guard would circle around with their horses at a walk, if it was a clear night and the cattle was bedded down and quiet, and one man would sing a verse of a song, and his partner on the other side of the herd would sing another verse; and you'd go through a whole song that way, like "Sam Bass." I had a crackerjack of a partner in '79. I'd sing and he'd answer, and we'd keep it up like that for two hours.[8]

In chapter 11 Abbott offered proof that being able to carry a tune was a valuable asset on Montana's open range some ninety years ago.

Cowboy author "Teddy Blue" Abbott (in the tall hat) poses with other old-timers at the Golden Jubilee celebration of the Montana Stock Growers' Association at Miles City in 1934. *Left to right:* Bill Hawkins, Abbott J. B. Hawkins, D. J. O'Malley, T. W. Longly.

> After we got up to the mouth of the Musselshell that fall, Newman (a cattleman) asked Johnny Burgess (his foreman) who he was keeping on for the winter and Burgess, starting to name them, said, "Teddy Blue." Newman said, "What are you keeping him for?"—because I was a new man.
>
> "Well," Burgess says, "he can sing."

Abbott adds that "old Newman snorted" but Burgess stuck to his guns and he kept the job.[9]

Will Croft Barnes, a rancher on northern Arizona's Little Colorado River for more than a quarter-century beginning in 1883, had an interesting slant on the business of night herders singing to the dogies. The following amusing bit is from his lengthy article on cowboy songs and singing that appeared in the *Saturday Evening Post* for June 27, 1925.

> Much has been written as to cowboy songs and the custom of singing to the cattle at night when on guard over the herd. It has been generally assumed that these musical efforts were meant to soothe the cattle with their sweet sounds. Far be it from me to discount the effect of music, no matter how crude or refined, upon a range cow's nerves. However, some thirty-odd years of cowboy life . . . have taught me to believe that the music has nothing to do with it. And if not the music, it certainly was not what theatrical and musical critics designate as the lyrics, which ran all the way from sacred hymns to some of the commonest doggerel imaginable. The simple fact is that no animals are more readily alarmed at night,

Alert for signs of trouble, a rider pauses to light up while circling a heard of sleeping cattle. The painting, by N. C. Wyeth, is from Philip Ashton Rollins, *The Cowboy*, published in 1922 by Charles Scribner's Sons. Used by permission of the publisher.

when in a mass, than the average range cattle. Let one's pony step on a small twig and break it with a sharp snap; or a wandering hoot owl, with raucous call, swoop down above the herd—whi-s-s-s-sh! Off they go, horns clashing, hocks rattling and heavy clouds of dust rising from their flying feet. . . .

Horses under the saddle for long hours are prone to shake themselves. No end of stampedes have had their origin because some tired cow pony, carrying a sleepy rider round the herd, gave himself a grand shake. A big cowboy saddle—with huge flappy tapaderos, a rope at the horn, thirty-inch leather skirts and a pair of saddle pockets hanging on each side—can, when properly shaken, kick up a noise fully equal to that produced by a tornado tearing off an old tin roof.

Not infrequently the rider lost his balance with this sudden upheaval underneath him and found himself sprawled flat on his back on the ground, his pony gone with the frightened cattle into the darkness and adding speed to their flying feet—the man trying hard to figure out how it all had happened. Therefore on a dark night any sudden or unusual sound is very likely to promote a stampede in a herd of range cattle; and by singing, the cowboys on guard merely furnish a cover to such noises—a counter-irritant, as it were.[10]

In the same article, Barnes tells of an Arizona cowboy, a Civil War veteran, who had learned one song, "Tenting Tonight," in the Union army.

. . . A few seasons on the Southwest ranges, however, and his war song had been changed to suit his new occupation. I can hear him now, jogging around a herd of steers in Northern Arizona on a dark night, singing away at the top of his fairly musical voice. He had the old tune all right, but the words badly mixed with local color:

> I'm a-ridin' tonight round this damn bed ground;
> Ridin' on a sore-backed hoss.
> An' I don't care a cuss what happens to the cows,
> For I'm gitten forty dollars an' found.
> Forty a month an' chuck-wagon grub,
> Forty a month an' found.
> Oh, think of the joys of a cowboy's life
> While you're ridin' round the old bed ground.[11]

NOTES

1. N. Howard Thorp, "Banjo in the Cow Camps," *Atlantic Monthly*, 166 (Aug., 1940), 199. For more on Thorp see chapter 19.

2. For D. J. O'Malley's comments on cowboy singing, see *Folklore of the Great West*, ed. John Greenway (Palo Alto, Calif.: American West Publishing Co., 1969), p. 195. Badger Clark's poem "A Bad Half Hour," describing an Arizona cowpuncher singing "Annie Laurie" on night guard, appears in all the numerous editions of his collected works titled *Sun and Saddle Leather*,

most recently issued in 1962 by the Westerners Foundation (Stockton, Calif.). For Wayne Gard's observations on daytime and nightime singing, see chapter 15 of *The Chisholm Trail* (Norman: University of Oklahoma Press, 1954). See also *The Story of the Cowboy* by Emerson Hough (New York: D. Appleton and Co., 1897), pp. 143–44. Owen Wister is quoted above, at the end of chapter 1; the most famous of all night-herding songs is discussed in chapter 5, "Move Slow, Dogies, Move Slow."

3. Ramon F. Adams, *The Old-Time Cowhand* (New York: Macmillan Co., 1961), p. 30.

4. J. Frank Dobie, *The Longhorns* (New York: Little, Brown and Co., 1941), p. 127.

5. John A. Lomax, *Adventures of a Ballad Hunter* (New York: Macmillan Co., 1947), p. 20.

6. J. Frank Dobie, "Cowboy Songs," *Country Gentleman*, Jan. 10, 1925, p. 9.

7. Walter Prescott Webb, *The Great Plains* (New York: Grosset & Dunlap, 1957), p. 459.

8. E. C. Abbott ("Teddy Blue") and Helena Huntington Smith, *We Pointed Them North: Recollections of a Cowpuncher* (1939; reprinted, Norman: University of Oklahoma Press, 1955), p. 223.

9. Ibid., p. 96.

10. Will Croft Barnes, "The Cowboy and His Songs," *Saturday Evening Post*, June 27, 1925, p. 14. Barnes is discussed in chapter 6.

11. Ibid.

5

Move Slow, Dogies, Move Slow

Oh, slow up, dogies; quit your rov-ing a-round. You've
wan-dered and tramped all o-ver the ground. Oh,
graze a-long, do-gies, and feed kind of slow, And don't for-
ev-er be on the go — Oh, move slow, do-gies, move_ slow. Hi-
yoo, hi-yoo-oo-oo, ____ Woo-oo-oo-oo-oo. ____

(falsetto)

Oh, slow up, dogies; quit your roving around.
You've wandered and tramped all over the ground.
Oh, graze along, dogies, and feed kind of slow,

And don't forever be on the go—
Oh, move slow, dogies, move slow.
   Hi-yoo, hi-yoo-oo-oo,
   Woo-oo-oo-oo-oo.

I've circle-herded, trail-herded, cross-herded, too;
But to keep you together, that's what I can't do.
My horse is leg-weary, and I'm awful tired;
But if I let you get away, I'm sure to get fired—
Bunch up, little dogies, bunch up.
   Yoo-oo-oo-oo-oo.
   Hey, cattle! Whoo-oop!

Oh, say, little dogies, when you going to lay down
And quit this forever sifting around?
My limbs are weary, my seat is sore;
Oh, lay down, dogies, like you've laid down before—
Lay down, little dogies, lay down.
   Hayyup, cattle! cattle!
   Hi-yoo, hi-yoo-oo-oo.

Oh, lay still, dogies, since you have laid down.
Stretch away out on the big open ground.
Snore loud, little dogies, and drown the wild sound—
They'll all go away when the day rolls 'round—
Lay still, little dogies, lay still.[1]

Texas cowpuncher Harry Stephens probably never thought of himself as a poet. In fact, he most likely would have gotten his back up had anyone called him that. But he certainly qualified for the club when he penned the accompanying word-picture of a tired rider slowly circling a herd of restless cattle in the darkness, singing to them, talking to them, begging them to lie down on the bed ground and sleep through the night. The famous "Night-Herding Song," which he composed in 1909 at the age of twenty-one, has stood the test of time. It has been quoted, usually as an anonymous contribution to western folklore, in virtually every anthology of poems and songs representative of American cowboy life.

Perhaps the appeal of Harry's one known effort at writing verse is due to its simplicity and directness. He gets down to business in the very first line. Possibly the questionable grammar in such lines as "Lay down, dogies, lay down" helps get across the feeling that these stanzas were written by a genuine working cowhand who spent his days on horseback, loved the out-of-doors, and never had much time for schoolrooms or book learning.

In his youth Harry was, indeed, as restless as the dogies he wrote

Harry Stephens (1888–1965) photographed in 1917 at Stoneman's Lake near Flagstaff, Arizona.

about. While still in his teens he left his birthplace, Denison, Texas, to roam Arizona and New Mexico, learning the cowboy's trade—breaking broncos, branding calves at the spring roundups, in the fall collecting beef cattle for shipping, taking his turn at night-herding. But to please his mother, he came back to Texas and at the end of the summer of 1908 enrolled at Texas A & M College at Bryan. He brought along his saddle trimmed with silver, his bridle, his spurs, and other cowboy gear, which he hung on the walls of his room. He slept in a bedroll instead of a bed. He often wore his boots and ten-gallon hat to class.

"Harry didn't like the college uniform," wrote John A. Lomax, a professor of English at Texas A & M at the time, "and he wasn't much interested in English literature, but he warmed up when I mentioned cowboy songs. He would stay after class and recite and sing songs to me." But when spring came in 1909, Professor Lomax reported in his autobiography, Harry appeared at the front gate of the Lomax home one morning and announced he was leaving. "Well, Professor," he said, "grass is rising—and I got to move on. I'm lonesome. I want to hear the wolves howl and the owls hoot."[2]

While Lomax never saw Harry Stephens again for many a year, during Harry's brief stay in the halls of ivy the two had developed a lasting friendship based on a common interest in the American cowboy song. Professor Lomax, deep in his project for rescuing and preserving the songs of the frontier, found Stephens an enthusiastic contributor of musical bits and pieces he had picked up in his travels. After leaving college, Harry often wrote Lomax and sent the words of additional songs he heard as his exciting career as a cowboy and rodeo contestant took him through California, Colorado, Arizona, Wyoming, Montana, and Idaho. Also among his unusual experiences was a job driving a stagecoach in Yellowstone National Park in the days before visitors did their sightseeing on rubber tires. He even had a brief fling at being a cowboy entertainer on the stage in California, in company with the great Will Rogers.

One day late in 1909 Lomax received an envelope from Harry containing a piece of a shoebox on which he had written the words of "Night-Herding Song."[3] Harry didn't say where he had obtained them, but he apologized for not being able to write out a tune he had made up for them. Professor Lomax guessed correctly that Harry had composed the verses himself. Furthermore, he felt that the words alone would make a valuable addition to the collection he was about to have published in his now-famous book titled *Cowboy Songs and Other Frontier Ballads*. So the words of "Night-Herding Song" were placed at the end of this volume, first printed in November, 1910, together with the notation "by Harry Stephens." "Night-Herding Song" was the only one of 112 in the book to carry the name of a cowboy composer. Lomax considered most of the others folk music, songs originated by forgotten cowpunchers, gold miners, stage drivers, or other unknown versifiers, and passed around from singer to singer, often being changed in the process, before being captured on the printed page.

Since Lomax was unable to supply music for "Night-Herding Song," anyone who spotted it in the Lomax book and wished to use it as a song was faced with making up his own tune. Strangely enough, the first person on record as having done so was a well-known English singer and composer, Liza Lehmann, who sixty-odd years ago created numerous musical arrangements for the London publishing firm of Chappell & Company. After a concert tour of the United States in 1910, Miss Lehmann compiled a song folio, ostensibly for the use of concert singers, with her own tunes and piano accompaniments for three poems that had been included, without music, in *Cowboy Songs and Other Frontier Ballads*—"The Rancher's Daughter" (titled "The Rambling Cowboy" by Lomax); "The Skew-Ball Black," a tale of a bucking horse; and "Night-Herding Song." In this folio Miss Lehmann used three out of four of Harry Stephens's stanzas, gave him full credit for the poem, explained correctly that the word *dogies* meant "cattle," but changed a few words and improved Harry's grammar for the benefit of British audiences. Here is her final stanza:

> Lie still now, since you have lain down,
> Stretch away on the big open groun';
> Snore loud, little dogies, and drown the wild sound,
> That will all pass away when the day rolls round,—
> Lie still, little dogies, lie still.[4]

To the best of my knowledge, it was not until 1928 that music for "Night-Herding Song" appeared in print in America, in a soft-cover collection called *Songs of the Open Range*.[5] Three years later, "Night-Herding Song," with a different and very lovely melody, was included in an outstanding hard-cover book, *Singing Cowboy*.[6] Since then it has turned up on the average of about once a year in printed song collections, in recent years enjoying wide popularity with publishers of songbooks for intermediate schools. While fairly faithful to Harry Stephens's original words, these books exhibit a wide variety of melodies, as do the versions of "Night-Herding Song" included on numerous phonograph records.

An oddity in the record field is one produced by that busiest of hillbilly singers, Texan Vernon Dalhart, who surprisingly included fewer than half a dozen old-time cowboy ballads among the approximately eight hundred songs that he recorded. In 1927 he made "Cowboy's Herding Song—Lay down, Dogies," sung in a minor key. This appears to be an imitation of the Stephens "Night-Herding Song" and was probably written by Dalhart himself. Here is the opening stanza:

> Oh, move slow, dogies, and lay down to rest,
> The sun is a-sinkin' out there in the West.
> Oh, move slow, dogies, stretch out on the ground,
> And don't be forever trampin' around.
> Move slow, dogies, move slow.
>   Hi-oh, hi-oh, hi-oh.[7]

The roving life of cowpuncher Harry Stephens ended in 1921. In 1917, while running his own herd of cattle on government-leased land forty miles south of Flagstaff, Arizona, he had met Elsie Miller, whose father was a cattle rancher near Mayer. Four years later the couple were married, after which they moved to Harry's home town of Denison, Texas, where he took over the management of a tree nursery business started long before by his father. At the same time he continued to work with cattle on a farm he acquired a few miles to the south.

A good many years later, in 1942 to be exact, Professor Lomax paid a visit to the Stephens household in Denison. He asked Harry for the story behind his "Night-Herding Song." Harry replied that he got the idea while he was working in Yellowstone National Park. As there was a shortage of hay for the horses that pulled the stages, the animals had to be turned loose to find grass. With no fences to hold them, someone had to ride herd on them to prevent their wandering away and becoming permanently lost. Here is the way Harry told it, according to John Lomax:

> Well, one summer I had a job herding a bunch of wild horses in Yellowstone Park at forty dollars a month. They were hard to hold, but I did the job so well the boss asked me if I would herd them nights at double my wages. That meant sixteen hours of hard riding out of twenty-four. At night I would get so sleepy I had to do something to keep awake. Those horses were always on the move, so I got to thinking I was riding round and round a herd of sleeping cattle and singing to keep them quiet. I'd make up a couple of lines and sing them to a sort of tune until I went into camp next morning, when I would write down the words. I meant it when I wrote:
>
> > I have circle-herded, trail-herded, cross-herded, too;
> > But to keep you together that's what I can't do.[8]

In 1946 the professor talked Harry into coming to the Lomax home in Dallas, where they held a recording session. Harry told the story of

Throughout his life, ex-cowpuncher Harry Stephens never felt at home without cattle or horses around. This photograph was taken about 1950.

the Yellowstone stage horses, then sang "Night-Herding Song" to his own tune, the one used at the beginning of this chapter. When, in 1952, the Music Division of the Library of Congress decided to issue a long-playing disc titled *Cowboy Songs, Ballads, and Cattle Calls from Texas* (L 28), Harry's conversation and his rendition of "Night-Herding Song" were included. For this he received a check for twenty-five dollars, his total cash take for his noted contribution to western music. In the credit department, too, he fared rather badly. Most of the editors of printed song collections that include "Night-Herding Song" appear never to have heard of Harry Stephens, even though his name was printed as big as life in the first Lomax volume more than sixty years ago and in several subsequent Lomax anthologies. Had these same editors cared to look, they would have found "Night-Herding Song," together with Harry's name, listed in that standard reference work, *Granger's Index to Poetry*, found in any fair-sized public library.

In September of 1947 Harry Stephens attended the eightieth birthday celebration for John Avery Lomax, where there was talk of the two of them making a trip together through the West, from Canada to Mexico, to glean more cowboy song material. This dream never developed into anything tangible; Lomax died only a few months later. In 1951 Harry discontinued his nursery business to give full time to his herd of cattle. He passed away in 1965 at the age of seventy-six.

NOTES

1. Richard E. Lingenfelter, Richard A. Dwyer, and David Cohen, *Songs of the American West* (Berkeley and Los Angeles: University of California Press, 1968), pp. 382–83. Transcribed by David Cohen from Harry Stephens's singing on *Cowboy Songs, Ballads, and Cattle Calls from Texas*, Library of Congress Archive of Folk Song L 28.

2. John A. Lomax, *Adventures of a Ballad Hunter* (New York: Macmillan Co., 1947), pp. 50–51.

3. *Houston Press*, Apr. 26, 1951.

4. Liza Lehmann, *Cowboy Ballads* (London: Chappell & Co., 1912).

5. Ina Sires, *Songs of the Open Range* (Boston: C. C. Birchard & Co., 1928), pp. 50–51.

6. Margaret Larkin, *Singing Cowboy* (1931; reprinted, New York: Oak Publications, 1963), pp. 10–12. Miss Larkin's version of "Night-Herding Song" was one of five English-language folksongs of the United States included by Charles Haywood in his book *Folk Songs of the World*, issued in 1966 by the John Day Company (New York), reissued in paperback in 1968 by Bantam Books (New York).

7. Victor 38455, Brunswick 138–A.

8. John A. Lomax, "The Singing Southwest," *Saturday Review*, May 16, 1942, p. 8.

6

Will Barnes and "The Cowboy's Sweet By and By"

Last night as I lay on the prairie,
And looked at the stars in the sky,
I wondered if ever a cowboy
Would drift to that sweet by and by.

The trail to that bright, mystic region
Is narrow and dim, so they say,
But the one that leads down to perdition
Is staked and is blazed all the way.

They say that there'll be a great round-up,
Where cowboys like dogies will stand,
To be cut by those riders from Heaven,
Who are posted and know every brand.

I wonder was there ever a cowboy
Pepared for that great judgment day,
Who could say to the boss of the riders,
I am ready to be driven away.

They say He will never forsake you,
That He notes every action and look,
But for safety you'd better get branded,
And have your name in His great tally-book.

For they tell of another great owner
Who is nigh overstocked, so they say,
But who always makes room for the sinner
Who strays from that bright, narrow way.

These verses, in later years known variously as "The Cowboy's Dream," "The Cowboy's Sweet By and By," and "Grand Roundup," appeared in the August, 1895, issue of *Cosmopolitan Magazine*. They were sung to the tune of "My Bonnie Lies over the Ocean" by the central character in a short story, "The Stampede on the Turkey Track Range," by Will Croft Barnes, soldier, rancher, author, editor, and conservationist. Thirty years later, writing in the *Saturday Evening Post* for June 27, 1925, Barnes gave the following interesting account of their origin:

> . . . I first heard this song in 1886 or '87 on the Hash Knife Range in Northern Arizona. A half-breed Indian boy from Southern Utah sang about four verses which he had picked up from some other singers. He knew nothing of the authorship. I wrote these four out in my calf-branding book one evening. Later on, a boy from down the Pecos way drifted into our camp and sang the four with slight variations, with two new ones, one of which he claimed as his own work. I wrote another and eventually picked up three more, until I finally had ten verses in all.
>
> With the idea of using it as a motif for a cowboy story, I rewrote two or three verses, changed the words of several, added the chorus, and cut the ten down to six verses. These were published with one of my earliest Western stories—The Stampede on the Turkey Track Range. So far as I have ever been able to run it down, this was the first time the words ever appeared in print. Since that time the song has been printed in almost every volume of cowboy songs which has been published.[1]

The chorus Barnes mentions never actually got into his *Cosmopolitan* story. However, it virtually always accompanies printed or recorded versions of the song. Sung to the chorus of "My Bonnie," it goes like this:

> Roll on, roll on, roll on, little dogies, roll on, roll on.
> Roll on, roll on, roll on, little dogies, roll on.

While I never met Will Barnes, I treasure a letter from him written in 1934, two years before Barnes died at the age of seventy-eight, in response to an inquiry about the history of this cattle-land allegory. Here is a portion of Barnes's reply: "I had sung it in public during the first political campaign I was in, in Arizona in 1888, when myself and another cow person made the campaign with a buckboard and a little folding organ which I played, and we sang cowboy and Mexican songs all over northern Arizona—and were terribly defeated at that. However, in 1890 we came back and were both elected to the legislature that year, with the same organ and songs."

As Austin and Alta Fife remark in their thorough discussion of "The Cowboy's Sweet By and By" in chapter 6 of *Songs of the Cowboys, by N. Howard ("Jack") Thorp*, "More than one cowboy poet has had a hand in the creation of this classic among night-herding songs,

A studio portrait of Will C. Barnes taken during his long career with the United States Forest Service.

and several more have tried to crown themselves with the glory of its creation."[2] Will Barnes, as he himself indicates, was, of course, in the first category. Whether the many variants of "The Cowboy's Sweet By and By" in print and on records today stem from his poetic editing, from the stanzas he heard others sing, or from other sources, no one knows. One thing we do know, however, is that the Barnes verses had a most curious later history. Publication in *Cosmopolitan* for August, 1895, was by no means the end of the line.

When he worked the song into his magazine story, Barnes made no mention of having composed any of its six stanzas. He simply had it sung by a cowhand on night guard who later met his death in a stampede. Because in the story Barnes referred to it as a "cowboy song" and made no claim to the authorship of any of the words, one Fred R. Reed, who wrote for a newspaper in Prosser, Washington, probably can be excused for borrowing five of the six stanzas and including them, almost word for word, in a discussion about the hereafter by two cowpunchers. This was headed "Cowboy Jack and the Angels" and went like this:

> "Last night as I lay on the prairie
> And looked at the stars in the sky,
> I wondered if ever a cowboy
> Would drift to that sweet bye and bye."

Jack laid his pipe down and, turning to his pard, who was also star gazing, said: "Old man, what do you think of that proposition, anyhow?"

"What's that, old boy?"

"Well, this deal about the sweet bye and bye. Do you think a couple of toughs like us would stand any kind of a show way up there among them angels, with their golden wings, the gold-paved streets, no end of harps, free music, everything coming your way, where everyone had his own private brand and the good Lord dead onto every angel in the herd? I've been sort of thinking this thing over, and it hits me bang in the short ribs that you and me had better sit in that kind of a game, play close and see if we can't win, for—

> "The trail to that bright, mystic region
> Is narrow and dim, so they say;
> But the one that leads down to perdition
> Is staked and blazed all the way.

"And that's dead right. It's no trouble to find the trail to hell; it's a cinch and you can't lose it, for the devil is the smoothest old boy in the deck. He sticks closer than that porous plaster I put on you that had been shot with bird shot. When the big round-up comes up we want to be easy to find.

"They say there will be a great round-up,
Where cowboys like cattle will stand—
To be cut out by those riders from heaven,
Who are posted and know every brand.

"Now, old sport, that verse is the apple dumpling of the whole lay out and shows that no monkeying goes for a minute. How are you going to get around it? You and me have been riding these ranges all our lives, and we ain't got a brand. We've got to croak some day. Look at pay-day; we get our dough and where is it? Booze—girls and booze! A scrap or two and we go back to work. It's the same old game, and you can't beat it. Do you think a cowpuncher *could* go to heaven, anyhow?

"I wonder was there ever a cowboy
Prepared for that great judgment day,
Who could say to the boss of the riders,
'I am ready to be driven away?'

"That last one is a hard crack. I don't see why a cowboy can't get there with both hoofs. I'm going to keep cases on them sky pilots and try to get onto their curves; but, old man, it's on the square and I know it. Listen to this:

"They say He will never forsake you—
That He notes ev'ry action and look;
But for safety you'd better get branded,
And have your name in His big tally book.

"Now you've got the whole snap right in the neck. I'm going to get branded. You had better shake off your hobbles and cash in your chips with me. When we get up yonder and jingle our spurs at the gate of the big corral and St. Peter looks out, we'll just tell his royal highness that we are the two biggest thoroughbreds that ever came from Turkey Track Range; that lately we've been on the dead square—no monkeying of any kind—and it's safe money that he'll say to some tenderfoot, 'Just fit these gentlemen out with wings.' Then we're in the game from that time on."

Fred Reed's piece was spotted by the editor of the *Northwest Magazine*, an influential monthly published at Saint Paul, Minnesota. He reprinted it in its entirety in his October, 1895, issue, with this introduction: "A bit of tender sentiment permeates every line in the following contribution to the Prosser (Wash.) *American* from the pen of Fred R. Reed."[3]

Readers of *Northwest* quite naturally would assume that Reed wrote the poetry as well as the prose. This left Will Barnes with only the satisfaction of knowing that through *Cosmopolitan* and *Northwest* many thousands of magazine readers had at least had the chance to peruse five stanzas of "The Cowboy's Sweet By and By" and possibly hum them to the tune of "My Bonnie Lies over the Ocean."

But that was not the end either. Two years later "Cowboy Jack and the Angels" turned up once more, in the weekly publication *Field and Farm* (Denver) for August 28, 1897. This time nobody received any credit.[4]

In 1908 Arizona author Sharlot Hall attempted to set the record straight. In her article "Songs of the Old Cattle Trails," written for the magazine *Out West*, she gave nine stanzas under the heading "The Cowboy's Sweet Bye and Bye," acknowledging the contribution of Will Barnes but adding that "every night-herding puncher from the Sonora line to the San Francisco Mountains had added a verse to suit himself."[5]

Miss Hall's first four stanzas were substantially the same as those used by Barnes in his *Cosmopolitan* short story. Her other five are given below. At first glance the last two of these resemble the last two used by Barnes. But on close examination, one sees that whereas with Barnes only the final stanza is an admonition to keep clear of the "bad place," in the Sharlot Hall version the last two have been interchanged and both used for issuing helpful advice to backsliding range hands.

> For they're all like the cows that are locoed,.
> That stampede at the sight of a hand,
> And are dragged with a rope to the round-up,
> Or get marked with some crooked man's brand.
>
> I know there's many a stray cowboy
> Who'll be lost at that great final sale,
> When he might have gone in to green pasture
> If he'd heard of that bright, mystic trail.
>
> And I'm scared I will be a stray yearling,
> A maverick, unbranded on high,
> And get cut in the bunch with the "rusties,"
> When the Boss of the Riders goes by.
>
> For they tell of another big owner,
> Who is ne'er over-stocked, so they say,
> But who always makes room for the sinner
> Who drifts from that straight, narrow way.
>
> And they say he will never forget you,
> That he knows every action and look;
> So for safety you'd better get branded—
> Have your name in the big Tally Book.[6]

Unique among the most popular of America's songs of the cattle trail because of its religious connotation, "The Cowboy's Sweet By and By" has found a place in virtually every printed collection of western

Twenty-seven-year-old Will Croft Barnes had been ranching for two years and had just had his first story accepted by the *Youth's Companion* when, in 1885, he struck this pose for a photographer in Prescott, Arizona. His army enlistment papers show that he was of extremely short stature—only five feet, four inches when he joined up in 1879. Photograph from the Arizona Historical Society, Tucson.

folksongs, beginning in 1908 with N. Howard "Jack" Thorp's first slim volume, *Songs of the Cowboys*. Thorp's five stanzas carried the title "Grand Round-up."

Numerous 78 rpm recordings of the song were on the market in the 1920s and '30s, the earliest having been made in 1924 by Charles Nabell (Okeh 40252-B) with the title "The Great Round-up." "The Cowboy's Dream," a version originally recorded in 1929 by Jules Verne Allen, was reissued in 1965 on a record in RCA Victor's Vintage series, *Authentic Cowboys and Their Western Folksongs* (LPV 522).

Born in San Francisco and raised in the Midwest, Will Croft Barnes went to Arizona in 1879 at the age of twenty-one as a soldier, a member of the Signal Corps. His assignment was military telegrapher at Fort Apache, soon to become a hot spot as Geronimo's warriors began their depredations that were to keep the territory in a turmoil five years. In September, 1881, the Apaches laid siege to the fort and cut its communications.

Barnes and a civilian scout volunteered to ride to Fort Thomas, about seventy miles to the south, for help. The scout, taking the usual wagon route, was killed. Barnes slipped through the besiegers, took a hill trail, and reached a ford over the Black River. Seeing an Indian camp nearby, he wrapped his horse's hooves with strips of blanket. The rushing water loosened the wrappings, and the Indians, alerted by the clatter of iron shoes on the rocks, began firing just as horse and rider clambered out on the far side. For getting the word through to Fort Thomas, Barnes received his country's highest military award, the congressional Medal of Honor.

The young soldier completed his enlistment in 1883 and went to ranching on the Little Colorado. Luck was with him again. He was fortunate enough to get established at a time when nature was good to Arizona cattlemen, in the lush days before the disastrous droughts of 1892 and 1893. During his career as a rancher he served in the territorial legislatures of both Arizona and New Mexico.

In 1907 Gifford Pinchot persuaded Barnes to leave his adopted Southwest and enter the infant United States Forest Service, where he served twenty-one years. One of his unusual achievements while in the Forest Service was helping to save the last of the Longhorns. After wrangling a small appropriation from Congress, Barnes and a companion traveled five thousand miles over the grassy plains and through the mesquite thickets of southern Texas rounding up remaining members of the historic breed then faced with extinction. Ten Longhorn cows and one bull were found in southwest Texas; ten cows, two bulls, and three steers were collected in the coastal area between Corpus Christi

At the age of seventy, Will C. Barnes again dons picturesque cowboy regalia, this time for a fancy dress ball given in December, 1929, by the United States Forest Service at Washington.

and Beaumont. The animals were shipped to the present Wichita Mountains Wildlife Refuge near Cache, Oklahoma, where three hundred of their descendants are on view today, a living monument to an exciting era of southwest history. Barnes described this unusual undertaking in the *Saturday Evening Post* for October 15, 1927.

Barnes also served on the United States Geographic Board, whose function is to investigate and authorize place-names and names of physical features for maps published in the United States. In 1931 he became associate editor of the fledging *Arizona Historical Review*, published by the University of Arizona.

A prolific writer for magazines, his first published work appears to have been "Raided by Apaches—A True Story of Cowboy Life in Arizona," printed in the *Youth's Companion* for October, 1885. Many writings in later years appeared in *Arizona Highways* and *Arizona Historical Review*.

Tales from the X-Bar Horse Camp, a collection of Barnes stories of Arizona range life including "The Stampede on the Turkey Track Range," was published in 1920 by *Breeder's Gazette* (Chicago). In collaboration with William McLeod Raine he wrote *Cattle*, issued in 1930 by Doubleday and reprinted in 1936 by Grosset & Dunlap with the title *Cattle, Cowboys and Rangers*. Although not exclusively about Arizona, this remains one of the best books written about the state's cattle industry. All through the volume there are snatches of songs, reflecting Barnes's lifelong interest in music.

When Barnes died in 1936 he left an unpublished autobiography, "Apaches and Longhorns." This was edited by his friend Dr. Frank C. Lockwood of Tucson and published in 1941 by the Ward Ritchie Press (Los Angeles).

In 1960 the University of Arizona Press issued *Arizona Place Names*, edited by Byrd H. Granger, a new and enlarged edition of a university bulletin authored by Barnes in 1935. The original work, long considered a classic in its field, was the culmination of a project on which Barnes spent many years. He described four thousand place names, gave the date when each post office was established, and listed the name of each postmaster.

Two years after Barnes died in Phoenix, where he resided after retiring from government service, two plaques designating Barnes Butte were dedicated in Papago Park. At Fort Huachuca, in 1958, the Will C. Barnes Memorial Field House was dedicated, and in 1964 his name was given to the Phoenix Army Reserve Center.

NOTES

An earlier version of this chapter appeared under the title "Will C. Barnes: Also a Song Plugger" in the *Arizona Republic* (Phoenix) Sunday supplement, January 14, 1968.

1. Will Croft Barnes, "The Cowboy and His Songs," *Saturday Evening Post*, June 27, 1925, p. 122.

2. Austin E. Fife and Alta S. Fife, *Songs of the Cowboys, by N. Howard ("Jack") Thorp* (New York: Clarkson N. Potter, Bramhall House, 1966), pp. 69–70.

3. *Northwest Magazine*, Oct., 1895, p. 14. This is the version quoted above.

4. *Field and Farm*, Aug. 28, 1897, p. 6. The full text of "Cowboy Jack and the Angels," reprinted from *Field and Farm*, also appears on pages 252–53 of *Trailing the Cowboy* (Caldwell, Idaho: Caxton Printers, 1955) by Clifford P. Westermeier, a professor of history at the University of Colorado.

5. Sharlot Hall, "Songs of the Old Cattle Trails," *Out West*, Mar., 1908, p. 217.

6. Ibid., p. 218.

7

D. J. "Kid" O'Malley, Montana Cowboy Poet

After the roundup's over,
After the shipping's done,
I'm going straight back home, boys,
Ere all my money's gone.
My mother's dear heart is breaking,
Breaking for me, that's all;
But, with God's help I'll see her,
When work is done this fall.

This is the story of a cowboy. His life was probably little different from that of thousands of other rugged men who grew up on the frontier and lived through Montana's memorable open range era of the 1880s and 1890s. But D. J. O'Malley, author of the well-known verse above, was a born communicator. And, like a few other genuine working cowpunchers such as Andy Adams and E. C. "Teddy Blue" Abbott, he left behind some choice word-pictures of a time long gone.

During the nineteen years he punched cattle in eastern Montana, O'Malley composed and published dozens of down-to-earth poems about cowboy life, several of which entered oral tradition and have become famous as folksongs of the American West. In later life, after he settled down in Wisconsin, his intense longing for the old days resulted in a series of historical articles, widely circulated in Treasure State newspapers during the 1930s, recalling the exciting days of Indian warfare and the subsequent romantic period when vast herds of Texas-born beef cattle dominated the landscape along the Missouri and the Yellowstone. As one who knew him during his last years, I welcome this opportunity to pay him belated tribute more than a century after his birth. Much of what is said here will be in his own words.

Dominick John O'Malley was born in New York City on April 30, 1867. His father, who had served with the Sixty-ninth New York Volunteers during the Civil War, reenlisted in the army but died in 1870 following an operation for the removal of a Confederate ball. His mother married another Union veteran, Charles White, who in 1876 moved his family to Fort Sanders, Wyoming Territory, and enlisted in the Second Cavalry, Troop E. One of White's first duties was to help bury the dead after the disastrous battle on the Little Big Horn on June 25, 1876.

Young O'Malley was ten years old when, in the summer of 1877, word came that the Second Cavalry was moving north from Fort Sanders to two new posts in Montana. Regimental headquarters would be at Fort Custer on the Big Horn, while four troops, including Troop E, would be stationed with the Fifth Infantry at Fort Keogh, under construction near the confluence of the Yellowstone and the Tongue. Accordingly, orders went out to the various Wyoming posts garrisoned by the Second for the troopers, baggage trains, and camp followers to rendezvous at Medicine Bow, forty miles northwest of Fort Sanders, for the arduous journey.

In 1936, in one of his many newspaper articles on early Montana history, D. J. O'Malley described this exciting expedition:

> By August 26th, 1877, the entire regiment with the exception of two troops already serving in Montana at Fort Ellis was in Medicine Bow awaiting orders to march into the Indian country. There were a great many children in the camp, many of the officers and enlisted men being married and their families traveling with them to the new country. To us children the camp was a scene of never-ending interest.
>
> Immediately after breakfast September 2 a trumpet sounded the call to break camp, and everyone sprang into action. About 9 o'clock the trumpet sounded "Assembly" and the different troops fell into position. Then with the call "Mount" they were in the saddle and the march started.[1]

The long column of horsemen and heavily loaded wagons forded the Platte at Fort Fetterman, where a soldier and two teams of mules were drowned in quicksand during the crossing. One overnight camp was made near the charred ruins of Fort Phil Kearny, burned by the hostiles in 1868 after being abandoned by the government. Fortunately, no redskins were encountered throughout the trip, although Indian scares were numerous. At a camp on Prairie Dog Creek, near

D. J. O'Malley (1867–1943) photographed in 1896 near Miles City, Montana.

the present site of Sheridan, Wyoming, the regiment came to the part-
ing of the ways—and a crisis. D. J. O'Malley described it:

The troops for Fort Custer began their journey the third morning
after we had pitched camp on Prairie Dog, and the Keogh contingent
were to leave the following morning. That night it was found that the
wife of a trumpeter of Troop E was in no condition to move for possibly a
week, and a new problem faced our commanding officer. It was decided
to leave our doctor and a detachment of soldiers at the camp while the
command went to Keogh from where an ambulance and other transportation were to be sent back for them. The commanding officer called for a
volunteer from among the women to stay with the sick woman and
though there were about twenty-five married women in our camp, my
mother was the only one who volunteered to stay. A detachment of
twenty-five men under command of my stepfather, Charles White, was
left to guard camp.

It was with misgivings that the little group watched the rest leave.
We were alone in a wild country overrun with hostile Indians and no one
knew when a war party would show up. Mrs. Clancy's baby was born that
night.

The evening of the sixth day after the troops had left us, we heard the
sound of a military trumpet from down the creek sound "Halt." White,
who was at the tents, ordered Clancy to sound "Advance," and the entire
camp was alive. In a minute or so, from across the creek came a body of
horsemen followed by a Red Cross ambulance and two four-mule jerk-
line teams. It was a detachment of soldiers from Keogh who had come for
us. One of the fort doctors, R. G. Redd, was with them and they had
medicine for the sick. Camp was lively that evening. We children had a
fine time with the new soldiers, who were from the Fifth Infantry. They
were mounted on captured Indian horses. Two of them were of our own
troops who had been sent with them as guides. Dr. Redd found that Mrs.
Clancy was in condition to be moved and the next day we started for Fort
Keogh. Mother went in the ambulance with Mrs. Clancy, while we children were placed in the wagons carrying camp equipment. We moved a
lot faster now than we had with the main command. After we struck the
Tongue River the country was smoother and the cavalry and all the
wagons were kept on a trot whenever practical.

On October 5 we came in sight of Fort Keogh, our future home. We
surely were an excited band of boys and girls. We went directly to the
new fort which was not yet entirely built, and the tents for the two
laundresses of troop E, my mother and Mrs. Clancy, were pitched about
200 yards east of the troop quarters. We stayed in tents all winter, as no
quarters had been built for the enlisted men's wives as yet. But all the
fine double frame buildings for the officers and their wives were about
completed.

Each married soldier had two 10 × 14 wall tents to live in. These were pitched, one directly in front of the other and both topped by a large government tarpaulin. They proved to be comfortable and we lived in ours until the following spring, when log houses were put up for the laundresses. These houses were built apart from the fort and were laid out in regular formation. The houses were about 50 feet apart with a back yard of 100 feet. There were about 65 of these dwellings in this section of Fort Keogh, which was known to the soldiers as Tub Town, and Sudsville, because most of the women who lived there were regular company laundresses.[2]

Fort Keogh, when the Second Cavalry arrived, was a busy place. Col. Nelson A. Miles, in command of the Fifth Infantry, the year before had built a cantonment at the junction of the Yellowstone and Tongue rivers and as soon as men and material could be obtained began building Fort Keogh. The cantonment was about two miles east of the new fort.

As I have said, the new fort was a busy place when we arrived. There was a small army of civilians there, carpenters, bricklayers, and the like, a great many quartermaster employees, packers and teamsters. Teams were coming and going all day hauling from the boat landing on the Yellowstone and from the cantonment, moving troops up as fast as quarters were finished. There were 14 companies of soldiers stationed there, the entire regiment of the Fifth Infantry and four troops of the Second Cavalry. Detachments of troops with either a string of pack mules or several wagons could be seen almost any day, either leaving the fort in pursuit of some raiding band of Indians or coming into the fort with a bunch of captives who were put in camp just west of the fort.

With Indian warfare continuing for several more years, the big army outpost on the Yellowstone was an intriguing place for a boy just entering his teens. Young O'Malley got to know many of the captive Indians who set up their village near the fort, and he naturally was on hand in June, 1881, when more than three thousand of them were loaded into stern-wheelers and shipped to Standing Rock Agency and points further south. And he, of course, knew young L. A. Huffman, later famed for his camera portraits of Indians and cowboys, who arrived from the East in 1879 to take over the job of post photographer.

But the fall of 1881 brought a calamity to the White family after four years at Keogh. Trooper Charles White disappeared. He had gotten into debt and was drinking heavily. When last seen he was headed in the direction of Canada on a saddle mule wearing Uncle Sam's brand. While he may have been "done in" by Indians, it was his stepson's opinion that he deserted.[3] At any rate, the former Margaret O'Malley was on her own once more.

It now became necessary to move from the fort into nearby Milestown (established in 1876) and for fourteen-year-old Dominick to turn to any work he could find to help support his mother and several sisters.

Under the circumstances there was little time for schooling. Moreover, getting an education in this raw frontier community had its difficulties. In a newspaper interview, D. J. O'Malley once stated that one never knew on leaving school in the afternoon where he would be attending the next day. School was held, he said, in whatever building happened to be available, and the trouble was none was available for that purpose for any length of time. For that reason the pupils usually carried home all their books and other classroom materials every night. He recalled going one morning to the building where he had attended school the day before and finding a saloon going full blast. The bartender told him he would find the school in so-and-so's livery stable, and there he found it.[4]

Within a year the youngster found work with a small cattle outfit organized by Captain T. H. Logan of the Fifth Infantry, father of two of O'Malley's chums at Fort Keogh. One of the first to see the possibilities for growing beef in eastern Montana, Logan shipped in 500 two-year-old heifers from Minnesota over the new Northern Pacific Railroad, branded them Anchor THL, and turned them loose on Little Dry Creek, where a crude ranch house had been built some sixty miles northwest of Miles. Young O'Malley—or Kid White, as he was known in those days—was hired as a horse wrangler.

Range scouts from Texas also were looking over the territory. In 1883 the Home Land & Cattle Company, owned by the Niedringhaus brothers, Saint Louis industrialists, bought Logan's herd and ranch. Shortly thereafter the first of many herds bearing the Niedringhaus brand, N-Bar-N, was driven up from west Texas to the company's new range. The young wrangler signed on with the new owners and was kept on through the winter to look after the horses. In due course he became an all-around cowhand and, with the exception of two short periods when he rode for the Bow-and-Arrow and the LU-Bar, was in their employ until 1896, when the Home Land & Cattle Company closed out its operation in Montana.

In another of his many newspaper articles, D. J. O'Malley described the broad scope of the Niedringhaus operation in the Treasure State:

> During the roundup season of 1886 they had eight crews or wagons on the range rounding up and shipping their cattle. They worked more men during the roundup season, worked their crews longer and fed their men better than the majority of cow outfits in the state. At the close of the season of 1886 it was estimated that the company had sixty-five thousand head of stock running on the range in Montana. Then came the disastrous winter of 1886–87, when range stock all over the northwestern ranges

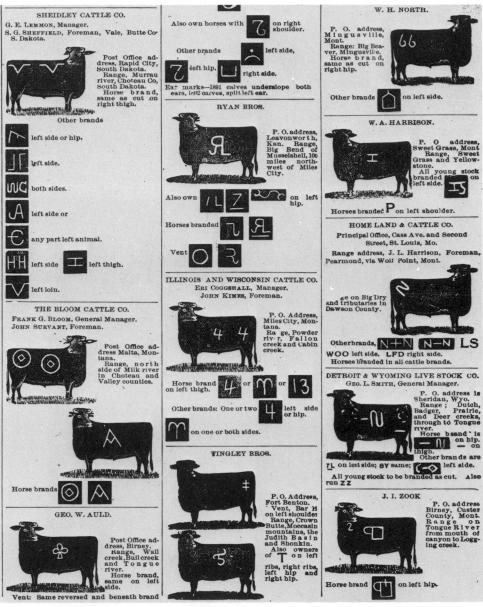

Miles City's weekly *Stock Growers' Journal*, which printed many of D. J. O'Malley's verses, always carried several pages of notices like those shown here from the issue for October 6, 1893. As cattle grazing on the open range often strayed far from home, stockmen advertised their brands widely. For a number of years O'Malley worked for the Home Land & Cattle Company, whose vital statistics are listed in the center of the right-hand column.

Sporting his first pair of chaps and his first six-shooter, a bone-handled one, D. J. O'Malley posed for this studio portrait at Miles City in 1884. He was seventeen and had just gone to work as a horse wrangler for the Home Land & Cattle Company.

perished in almost countless numbers, and the N-Bar-N, like almost every other stock owner, lost heavily.

At the close of the general roundup in the spring of 1887 it was found that the loss to the N-Bar-N was between forty thousand and forty-five thousand head. But this terrific loss did not deter the Niedringhaus brothers. They immediately began to put up herds in the south to be driven north to their depleted range in Montana, and for several years almost every other herd that was driven over the trail to Montana bore the road or trail brand of the N-Bar-N, and in the years of 1891, '92 and '93 they were reputed as paying taxes on one hundred thousand head of cattle in the three counties of Custer, Dawson and Valley.

The stock of the N-Bar-N ranged over an immense scope of country. Riders who were sent out as "reps" to work with outfits off the home range were often with wagons over 100 miles from the home ranch and found N-Bar-N cattle. In 1893 the writer, riding as a "rep," worked with Wyoming wagons and shipped beeves for the company from Suggs, Wyoming, nearly two hundred miles from the home ranch.

In 1893, from statistics taken from the books of Clay Robinson Co., and Rosenbaum, Bros., commission firms in Chicago, it was found that the Home Land & Cattle Co. had shipped to the Chicago stockyards twenty-three thousand head of beef cattle in the shipping season of that year. This was the largest number of beef cattle ever shipped from the northwestern range by one concern at any time.

Many outfits came to Montana from Texas after 1886 but ninety-nine per cent of the cattle that were driven in were steers instead of cows. Among these outfits were the XIT, Circle Diamond, and Diamond A. The winter of 1886 taught them that though Montana could not be beaten as a beef raising country, it was not a good range whereon to raise calves, and they profited by the experience of those that lost so heavily during that ill-fated winter.[5]

His long term of service as a "rep"—short for *representative*—for the N-Bar-N brand was a great source of pride to D. J. O'Malley. His friend "Teddy Blue" Abbott, son-in-law of pioneer cattleman Granville Stuart and author in 1939 of the cowboy classic *We Pointed Them North*, was proud of it, too. Many years ago "Teddy Blue" published the following pat on the back for his fellow cowpuncher, together with an explanation of the "rep's" function in the range cattle business:

The fact that he was sent out to "rep" is enough to prove that he was a good cowpuncher and was trusted by his wagon boss. Charlie LeNoir told me one day that you could sure tie to Kid White, and that is the greatest compliment you could pay to a man on the range. A "rep" had to be a good fellow, a good mixer, and he had to be good on brands, and above all loyal to his outfit, and they all were; they had to be or leave the range. Believe me, it was no picnic repping for those big outfits, as they were always putting in cattle and ran all kinds of brands, and some of the men had to rep for a whole range, but they hardly ever overlooked a bet. Always well mounted, no "rep" would start out with a poor string. They would pack their bed and warbag on a gentle horse and string out. Some were gone all summer and would go hundreds of miles from the home ranch. Their word was law in regard to all the cattle they represented, calves branded and the beef shipped. "Reps" saved their outfits thousands of cattle. They were honest as day, would fight for their outfit any time. In fact, any cowpuncher would.[6]

Early in his career as a cowboy, D. J. O'Malley developed a knack for writing verse. Fortunately, he wrote mostly about his own experiences and those of others who followed the cowpuncher's rough and often dangerous trade. As a result he left some excellent descriptions of that long-vanished era when one could ride to the top of a ridge and see virtually nothing in either direction but cattle and horses.

During the nineteen years he rode the range in eastern Montana, O'Malley composed scores of verses about everything under the sun, from Miles City's Old Gray Mule Saloon to advice for would-be sheepherders, from praise for his favorite cow horse to an endorsement of the McKinley-Roosevelt ticket. He even got into the 1894 battle between Anaconda and Helena over the location of the Montana capital, supplying one faction with a song entitled "After the Fall," to be sung to the tune of the then-popular "After the Ball." That he was betting on the wrong horse is evident from his chorus, in which he takes a dig at the elite of Helena who frequented the nearby resort built in 1889 by Colonel C. A. Broadwater:

> After the Fall is over,
> After the voting's done,
> There will be great rejoicing
> When Anaconda's won.
>
> Helena with her Four Hundred
> Won't be on the map at all.
> They'll eat crow at the Broadwater
> After the Fall.[7]

Many O'Malley verses were printed in the *Stock Growers' Journal*, a few in the *Yellowstone Journal*, both published in Miles City. His earliest contribution that can be tied down to a definite date is an amateurish six-stanza piece about a 4–4 cowboy named Wiley Collins who was killed by lightning on a roundup. It was carried in the *Stock Growers' Journal* on August 3, 1889, and signed D. J. White (he appears to have used his stepfather's family name until he was in his thirties). On another page of the same issue there is a brief news note:

Cowboy minstrels Pete Jacobi and Charlie Jackson pose for D. J. O'Malley's camera at the J P Ranch in eastern Montana, September, 1904.

"Kid White was in town during the week." The implication is that the budding twenty-two-year-old range poet delivered his work to the newspaper office in person and used his Irish charm on the editor.

Two years later, on July 11, 1891, the *Journal* published another verse written in the same vein but sporting a bit more polish. Called "A Cowboy's Death" and signed with the initials D.J.W., it describes the tragic end of a hand named Charlie Rutledge who rode for the XIT, the giant Texas outfit which early in 1890 leased two million acres of range between the Yellowstone and Missouri rivers.[8] The author told me he wrote this to fit the tune of an old song called "The Lake of Pontchartrain."

This is one of several O'Malley ballads which found favor with his fellow cowpunchers and, as the folklore experts say, "entered oral tradition," meaning it was passed along from one singer to another over many years with no clue as to its origin. Professor John A. Lomax picked it up in Texas, with slight variations, and included the words in his famous book *Cowboy Songs and Other Frontier Ballads*, first published in 1910. The title here is "Charlie Rutledge." It also appeared, with music, in *Songs of the Open Range*, compiled in 1928 by Ina Sires, a Dallas schoolteacher. But perhaps the greatest compliment ever paid these verses was by the eminent American composer Charles

Ives, in 1947 winner of the Pulitzer Prize for music, who ran across the poem in the Lomax book and prepared an elaborate arrangement for voice and piano, published initially by G. Schirmer in 1921.[9]

Here is the original poem from the pages of the *Journal*—a rather handsome epitaph when one realizes that many a cowboy killed in line of duty was lucky to get two lines in a local newspaper. The "Kid White" mentioned in the second stanza obviously is not our cowboy poet:

> Another good cowpuncher
> Has gone to meet his fate;
> We hope he'll find a resting place
> Inside the golden gate.
> A good man's place is vacant
> At the ranch of the X I T,
> And 'twill be hard to find one who
> Was liked as well as he.
>
> First Kid White of the Flying E,
> Then Preller, young and brave,
> Now Charlie Rutledge makes the third
> That has been sent to his grave
> By a cow-horse falling on him
> Whilst running after stock
> This Spring, while on the roundup,
> Where death a man does mock.
>
> How blithely he went forth that morn
> On the circle through the hills,
> Happy, gay and full of life
> And free from earthly ills;
> And when they came to clean the bunch,
> To work it he was sent,
> Not thinking that his time on earth
> Was very nearly spent.
>
> But one X I T would not go
> And turned back in the herd,
> So Charlie shoved him out again,
> His cutting horse he spurred;
> Another started to come back,
> To head him off he tried,
> The creature fell, the horse was thrown,
> And 'neath him Charlie died.
>
> 'Twas a sad death for man to meet
> Out on that lonely lea;
> His relatives in Texas live,

No more his face they'll see;
But we hope the Father greets him
With a smile upon his face,
And seats him by his right hand
Near the shining throne of grace.

A third poem dealing with a fatal accident during a roundup, published in the *Stock Growers' Journal* for October 6, 1893, has earned O'Malley considerable fame in folklore circles. This is "After the Roundup," whose chorus appears at the beginning of this chapter. Variants of this, with the title "When the Work's All Done This Fall," have been widely circulated through printed song collections and phonograph records. A Victor 78 rpm recording made in 1925 by Texan Carl Sprague sold more than nine hundred thousand copies.[10]

Best known of all O'Malley's poetic efforts, "After the Roundup" was written to fit the tune of the Charles Harris waltz-time song hit of 1892, "After the Ball," whose refrain, beginning "after the ball is over," is often heard even today. The O'Malley ballad began:

A group of jolly cowboys
Discussed their plans at ease,
Said one: "I'll tell you something
Boys, if you please:
See, I'm a puncher,
Dressed most in rags,
I used to be a wild one
And took on big jags.

I have a home boys,
A good one, you know,
But I haven't seen it
Since long, long ago.
But I'm going home, boys,
Once more to see them all:
Yes, I'll go back home
When work is done this fall."

Repenting of his wild and spendthrift ways, the cowboy vows to "walk the straight path" and return to his brokenhearted mother. But it is not to be. That very night the cattle stampede, his horse stumbles and crushes him. As he lies dying he speaks to his fellow punchers:

"Bill, take my saddle,
George, take my bed,
Fred take my pistol
After I am dead.
Think of me kindly
When on them you look—"
His voice then grew fainter,
With anguish he shook.

His friends gathered closer
And on them he gazed,
His breath coming fainter,
His eyes growing glazed.
He uttered a few words,
Heard by them all:
"I'll see my mother
When work's done this fall."

Today no one uses the old Charles Harris tune for the song, but the story, with the exception of the last few lines, has survived in just about the form O'Malley wrote it in 1893. As it went the rounds in the West, some anonymous rhymester gave the subject of the ballad a name

—Charlie—and an epitaph, neither of which he had in the O'Malley original. Here is the way it ends in the well-known version given by John A. Lomax in *Cowboy Songs*:

> Poor Charlie was buried at sunrise, no tombstone at his head,
> Nothing but a little board and this is what it said,
> "Charlie died at daybreak, he died from a fall,
> And he'll not see his mother when the work's all done
>   this fall."[11]

It was through an incident connected with this particular song that I met D. J. O'Malley. As a moonlighting singer of western ballads over New York radio stations, I was always on the lookout for background material on my songs. In 1932, in the January 23 issue of Street & Smith's *Western Story Magazine* I spotted a letter from him complaining about one R. O. Mack whose name appeared as author and composer of "When the Work's All Done in the Fall," published in sheet music in 1929 by the now-defunct F. B. Haviland Music Publishing Company of New York. The magazine obligingly ran the *Stock Growers' Journal* version in its entirety. I immediately sent off a letter to Eau Claire, Wisconsin, where O'Malley had lived most of the time since leaving Montana, and we entered into a voluminous correspondence which kept up for years.

All through this correspondence, there are references to R. O. Mack. Every time O'Malley thought of this "poem rustler"— actually a fictitious character—his blood pressure went up. Seeing in print "Words and music by R. O. Mack" bothered him much more than the fact that for a while phonograph records of his brainchild were selling like hot cakes and he never got a nickel out of it.

In 1933 I was able to visit Eau Claire and examine the old cowpuncher's unusual scrapbook. From then on I was able to help him obtain at least a little credit for his contribution to western American folklore. I brought his work to the attention of John Lomax, who also began corresponding with him and thought enough of his claims to authorship to mention him three times in the revised and enlarged edition of *Cowboy Songs*, issued in 1938 and reprinted many times.[12]

I failed to make any impression, however, on another folklore notable from the Lone Star State—the late J. Frank Dobie. For the record, I have to say that he considered D. J. O'Malley a johnny-come-lately. In spite of O'Malley's having published a stack of verses and having written many more that never saw print, Dobie maintained he could not have composed the songs under discussion here, that they were much older. And to him, a cowboy song as genuine as "When the

Work's All Done This Fall" could have originated in only one place—Texas.[13]

Not all of O'Malley's poetic efforts were as doleful as those given above. On February 3, 1894, the *Stock Growers' Journal* published an extremely humorous yarn called "The 'D2' Horse Wrangler" that can be found in many printed collections and on records under the titles "The Tenderfoot" and "The Horse Wrangler." In the *Journal* the verses are signed R. J. Stovall. O'Malley told me he himself wrote them but because the subject wanted to surprise his wife by blossoming out as a poet, he was allowed to sign his name, for a consideration—a five-dollar hat—which was the most O'Malley ever received for a set of verses. He said the poem was written to fit the tune of a popular comic Irish-American song, "The Day I Played Base Ball," composed by the first Pat Rooney, a vaudeville star of the 1880s.

Below are the words of "The 'D2' Horse Wrangler" as published in the *Stock Growers' Journal*. The "Macqueen" mentioned in the opening stanza was the largest hotel in Miles City and headquarters for stockmen. At the time, its newspaper advertising was playing up its electric lights, electric bells, and steam heat.

Considering the general excellence of the rhyming, the poor rhyme in the third line of the second stanza probably can be laid to a

Says He: "My foreman is in town;
He's at the Macqueen, his name is Brown."

An L. A. Huffman photograph of the Macqueen mentioned in the poem "The 'D2' Horse Wrangler." Erected at Miles City in 1882, in 1907 it went up in smoke.

Catcher on the Miles City nine from 1889 through 1893, versatile D. J. O'Malley models the latest in diamond togs. His famous poem "The 'D2' Horse Wrangler" was set to the tune of "The Day I Played Base Ball," the opening stanza of which, from *Pat Rooney's Claribel Magee Songster* (New York: A. J. Fisher, 1882), p. 18, reads as follows:

My name it is O'Halloher,
I'm a man that's influential,
I mind my business, stop at home,
My wants are few an' small,
Some blackguards 'tother day did come,
They were full of whiskey, gin and rum,
An' they took me out in the broilin' sun,
To play a game of ball.

printer's unsuccessful effort to decipher a handwritten manuscript.
The writer obviously meant to say "He said cowpunching was only
play."

The term *cavard* in the third stanza of the poem is a corruption of a
Spanish word, *caballada*, for a herd of horses. A *set fast* (fifth stanza)
means, in cowboy vernacular, a saddle sore that never quite heals.

The first stanza is set to the tune of "The Day I Played Base Ball"
as printed in the *New York Mercury* for Sunday, April 10, 1892, with
this notation: "Composed and sung by the late Pat Rooney, Copyright
1878 by E. H. Harding."

One day I thought I'd have some fun,
And see how punching cows was done;
So, when the roundup had begun,
I tackled a cattle king;
Says he: "My foreman is in town;

He's at the Macqueen, his name is Brown;
Go over, and I think he'll take you down";
Says I: "That's just the thing."

We started for the ranch next day,
Brown talked to me 'most all the way,
He said cow punching was only fun,
It was no work at all;
That all I had to do was ride,
It was just like drifting with the tide,
Geemany crimany, how he lied;
He surely had his gall.

He put me in charge of a cavard
And told me not to work too hard,
That all I had to do was guard
The horses from getting away.
I had one hundred and sixty head,
And oft' times wished that I were dead,
When one got away Brown he got red.
Now this is the truth, I say.

Sometimes a horse would make a break
And across the prairie he would take
As though he were running for a stake,
For him it was only play.
Sometimes I couldn't head him at all
And again my saddle horse would fall
And I'd speed on like a cannon ball
Till the earth came in my way.

They led me out an old gray hack
With a great big set fast on his back,
They padded him up with gunny sacks
And used my bedding all.
When I got on he left the ground
Jumped up in the air and turned around
I busted the earth as I came down,
It was a terrible fall.

They picked me up and carried me in
And rubbed me down with a rolling pin:
"That's the way they all begin,
You are doing well," says Brown,
"And to-morrow morning, if you don't die,
I'll give you another horse to try."
"Oh! wont you let me walk?" says I,
"Yes," says he, "into town."

I've traveled up and I've traveled down,
I've traveled this country all around,
I've lived in city, I've lived in town,
And I have this much to say;
Before you try it go kiss your wife,
Get a heavy insurance on your life,
Then shoot yourself with a butcher knife,
It's far the easiest way.

In addition to the songs which have lasted so long because of their universal appeal—and, I suppose, because they were good songs—there are several O'Malley poems, printed once, then apparently forgotten, which seem worth republishing here because they mirror some interesting facets of life in the unique period of American frontier history.

One called "The Cowboy Wishes" appeared in the *Journal* for April 7, 1894, signed D. J. White.[14] The author said he wrote it while the Stock Growers' Association was meeting in Miles City and the town was full of young fellows seeking jobs as cowhands. He explained that "to make some Winter plays" (first stanza) meant to keep busy while in sight of the boss so as to be in line when the scarce off-season jobs were doled out. Those who failed to make the grade might have to turn to the cold, lonely job of trapping wolves for bounty money. To "catch a regular" meant to take a nap on day herd while the cattle were lying around on water.

I want to be a cowboy
And with the cowboys stand,
With leather chaps upon me
And a six-gun in my hand.
And, while the foreman sees me
I'll make some Winter plays,
But I will catch a regular
When the herd's thrown out to graze.

I'll have a full-stamped saddle
And a silver-mounted bit,
With conchos big as dollars,
And silvered spurs, to wit;
With a long rawhide reata
And a big Colt's forty-five
I'll be a model puncher
As sure as you're alive.

I want to be a tough man,
And be so very bad,

With my big white sombrero
I'll make the dude look sad.
I'll get plumb full of bug juice
And shoot up the whole town
When I start out to have a time,
You bet I'll do it brown.

I want to be a buster
And ride the bucking horse,
And scratch him in the shoulders
With my silvered spurs, of course.
I'll rake him up and down the side,
You bet I'll fan the breeze.
I'll ride him with slick saddle
And do it with great ease.

I want to be a top man
And work on the outside
So I can ride within the herd
And cut it high and wide.
Oh, a rep is what I want to be,
And a rep, you bet, I'll make.
At punching cows I know I'll shine;
I'm sure I'll take the cake.

"A Busted Cowboy's Christmas" first appeared in the Miles City *Stock Growers' Journal* for December 23, 1893. O'Malley got the idea for these verses, he told me, on a winter night after he had been separated from two dollars by a busted cowboy with a long spiel. He said that although he himself seldom lacked winter employment during the entire nineteen years he cowboyed in Montana, there were many young fellows who were only good enough to fill in as herders during the roundups and were no longer needed in the late fall after the beef cattle had been shipped to market. O'Malley signed the verses Iyam B. Usted, which was entirely in character with this imaginative Irishman. On another occasion he sent an account of a cowboy dance at Rosebud, Montana, to a Miles City paper, listing himself among the guests and signing the article Jack R. Abbit.

I am a busted cowboy
And I work upon the range
In summer time I get some work
But one thing that is strange,
As soon as fall work's over
We get it in the neck
And we get a Christmas present
Of a neatly written check.

STOCK GROWERS' JOURNAL

SUBSCRIPTION IN ADVANCE.

One Year. ....$3 | Three Months. 1
Six Months........ 2 | Single Copies. 10c
Foreign Subscriptions. Single Number. $4.

Published Every Saturday at Miles City.

Entered at the Post-office in Miles City, Montana, as Second-Class Mail Matter

ADDRESS ALL COMMUNICATIONS TO

BUTLER & POTTER.

Editors and Proprietors

SATURDAY. DECEMBER 23, 1893.

A Busted Cowboy's Christmas.

I am a busted cowboy
And I work upon the range
In summer time I get some work
But one thing that is strange,
As soon as fall work's over
We get it in the neck
And we get a christmas present
Of a neatly written check

Then come to town to rusticate,
We've no place else to stay,
While winter winds are howling loud,
Cause we can't eat hay.
A puncher's life's a picnic (?)
It is one continued joke,
But there's none more anxious to see spring
Than a cowboy who is broke.

The wages that a cowboy earns
In summer goes like smoke,
And when the winter snows have come
You bet your life he's broke
You can't talk about your holiday,
Your Christmas cheer and joy,
It's all the same to me, my friend,
Cash gone—I'm a broke cowboy.

My saddle and my gun's in soak
My spurs I've long since sold,
My rawhide and my quirt are gone,
My chaps—no, they're too old,
My stuff's all gone, I can't e'en beg
A solitary smoke.
For no one cares what becomes of
A cowboy who is broke.

Now, where I'll eat my dinner
This Christmas, I don't know,
But, you bet I'm going to have one
If they give me half a show.
This Christmas has no charms for me,
On good things I'll not choke,
Unless I get a big hand-out,
I'm a cowboy that is broke.

IYAM B. USTED.

Then come to town to rusticate,
We've no place else to stay,
While winter winds are howling loud,
Because we can't eat hay.
A puncher's life's a picnic (?)
It is one continued joke,
But there's none more anxious to see spring
Than a cowboy who is broke.

The wages that a cowboy earns
In summer goes like smoke,
And when the winter snows have come
You bet your life he's broke.
You can talk about your holiday,
Your Christmas cheer and joy,
It's all the same to me, my friend,
Cash gone—I'm a broke cowboy.

My saddle and my gun's in soak
My spurs I've long since sold,
My rawhide and my quirt are gone,
My chaps—no, they're too old,
My stuff's all gone, I can't e'en beg
A solitary smoke.
For no one cares what becomes of
A cowboy who is broke.

Now, where I'll eat my dinner
This Christmas, I don't know,
But, you bet I'm going to have one
If they give me half a show.
This Christmas has no charms for me,
On good things I'll not choke,
Unless I get a big hand-out,
I'm a cowboy that is broke.

While riding for the N-Bar-N, D. J. O'Malley went south three times to drive herds north to Montana. The windup of his last trip inspired a set of verses called "Cowboy's Soliloquy" published by the *Stock Growers' Journal* on November 28, 1891, and signed D. J. White. Here is his explanation, from a letter written to me in 1934:

I was with a trail herd from the Texas Panhandle in 1891. We left the Canadian River in early March and crossed the Yellowstone onto the N-Bar-N range the middle of September. We were to drive them to the Little Dry and turn them loose, but two days before we got to where we were to ride off from them we got word to hold them along the Little Dry until further orders. We didn't get away from them until the 14th of

In winter camp near Miles City, 1894, D. J. O'Malley and his horse, Chromo, have good reason to look tired. The pair of them had put in a hard day pulling cattle out of a bog.

October—just about eight months looking at the same dogies. Every day grew so monotonous we scarce knew what to do with ourselves. Just day herd and night guard.

Along with the excellent picture of frustration given in "Soliloquy," the reader will note the word *dogies* in the first and third stanzas. To the best of my knowledge, this is the earliest date (1891) that this expression, which undoubtedly originated in Texas, appeared in print. As to *how* it originated, I have seen half a dozen explanations. The late J. Frank Dobie once put it this way: "By dogie is meant a little calf as well as motherless calf, and the term is often applied to yearlings and even to cattle in general." [15]

> I am a cowpuncher
> From off the North Side,
> My horse and my saddle
> Are my bosom's pride;
> My life is a hard one,

Git Along, Little Dogies

To tell you I'll try
How we range-herded dogies
Out on the Little Dry.

The first thing in the morning
We'd graze upon the hill,
Then drive them back by noontime
On water them to fill,
Then graze them round till sundown,
And I've heaved full many a sigh
When I thought "two hours night guard"
After night fell on the Dry.

The next day was the same thing
And the next the same again,
Day-herding those same dogies
Out on the Dry's green plain;
Grazing them, then bedding them,
One's patience it does try
When you think "now comes our night guard"
After night falls on the Dry.

They're all right in the daytime,
But our Autumn nights are cold,
And the least scare will stampede them,
And then they're hard to hold.
How many times I've "darned" the luck
When dusk I would see nigh,
And say, "I wish you were turned loose
E're night falls on the Dry."

For a large bunch of cattle
Is no snap to hold at night,
For sometimes a blamed coyote howl
Will jump them in a fright,
Then a man will do some riding,
O'er rocks and badlands he will fly;
A stampede is no picnic
After night falls on the Dry.

Then should my horse fall down on me
And my poor life crush out,
No friendly hand could give me aid,
No warning voice could shout;
They'd hardly give one thought to me
Or scarcely heave a sigh,
But they'd bury me so lonely
When the night fell on the Dry.

D. J. O'Malley photographed at Billings, Montana, in 1903, while serving as a deputy stock inspector.

A Montana cowboy's life was not all ridin' and ropin'. Here D. J. O'Malley takes time out from other roundup chores for a turn at the old washtub. The picture was taken in 1900.

After the Niedringhaus brothers sold out—to McNamara and Marlow in 1896—O'Malley rode for the M-Diamond and Quarter Circle L brands, both on the Tongue River, served three years as a deputy stock inspector under Billy Smith, was a deputy sheriff for a while, then rode for the 79 brand on the Musselshell and the Hog Eye on Cabin Creek. Again quoting "Teddy Blue": "Kid White saw as hundreds of others did, that the game was about played out, and he went to Deer Lodge (the state penitentiary) and was a guard there under Frank Conley for two years. Tiring of that, he drifted east and there a pretty girl got her rope on him and broke him plumb gentle, and he never fought the rope either."[16]

O'Malley's story is that after he married Mary Manchester in Wisconsin, in 1911, he intended to go back to Deer Lodge but he just didn't, at least not until 1921 when a new warden, M. W. Potter, who was an old friend, enticed him back for another stint, three years this time. He considered he played somewhat of a practical joke on the younger of his two daughters by allowing her to be born at the penitentiary. Before settling down again in Wisconsin, he worked for short periods as a policeman in Aberdeen, South Dakota, and as a streetcar motorman in Minneapolis.

As I have said, when our paths first crossed, in 1932, D. J. O'Malley was living in Eau Claire. He was a raspberry farmer and, ironically, was working in a factory that made tires for the machine that put the horse out of business. But his heart was still in Montana. When a real bad spell of homesickness hit him, he wrote another poem, or a historical article for a book he hoped to publish, or sent me a long letter about the old days, quite often packed with sly humor. I have one of these dated December 2, 1935, commenting on a feature story about his cowboy career that had been run in the Eau Claire newspaper:

Since that article showed up I've been asked a million questions about the range, cows, cowboys, etc. And some of the damndest fool questions you ever heard. For instance. When you are on night herd where do you get the bedding for such a big herd of cattle every night? How many acres does a big cattle company have to have to hold all their cattle? But the question I am asked the most is: "What is a rep and what does he do?" It gets tiresome and yet it is amusing. I told one persistent woman, as to the bedding, that we always had a crew with mowing machines that were two days ahead of the herd. They always knew where we would camp each night and would have grass enough cut for the purpose. The cook and the horse wrangler would spread it on the ground just before sundown. Honestly, I believe she really believed it, for she seemed fully satisfied.

A second letter, dated December 15, contains more of the same:

> I am having more fun than a little on account of that article in the paper. Honest, I didn't think people could be so ignorant. I am asked such fool questions personally, by telephone and even by mail. Here is one question I've been asked several times: Don't it hurt a calf to brand it? Another: Does the same calf have to be branded every spring? What do you think of those? I told one fellow (a full grown man) if he would sit in his bare skin on a red hot stove for a minute he could form a good idea as to how a calf felt when a hot iron was putting a brand on its side. Doggone if I don't get out of patience with some of them. One lady asked me in all good faith who milked all the cows a cow outfit owned. It's sure funny.

O'Malley's ability to make a joke under the most trying circumstances is demonstrated in a letter written December 12, 1936:

> I hope that this letter will find you all well. I can't say it leaves me in that condition. I have been under the doctor's care for three weeks and have been cooped up in the house all that time, most of it in bed, and I don't know when I will be able to go back to work again—probably never—as my heart is in a bad way and the doctor says my kidneys are pretty badly affected, and that's no good way to be with winter here and coal $12 a ton and groceries climbing in price. Not a very cheerful outlook for the old hand, I must say, but I guess I will pull through. If I don't it will be a case similar to that of the Dutchman's horse when it died. It will be the first time that ever happened.

During the last decade of his life, D. J. O'Malley managed to get back to his beloved Montana three times. The first was in 1934, when Miles City celebrated the fiftieth anniversary of the founding of the Montana Stock Growers' Association. Eau Claire's retired cowpuncher attended through the generosity of John Lair of Chicago's radio station WLS. Lair had had the cowboy poet on several programs both in Chicago and at Renfro Valley, Kentucky, and also arranged to have his poem "The Dying Rustler" recorded by singer Red Foley (Conqueror 8198).

In 1939 he went again, as one of three veteran riders from the roundup of 1881 present at a cowboy reunion. The third but not actually the last trip to his old range was in 1941, two years before his death. It was for a reunion of the newly organized Range Riders Association and dedication of a cowboy museum. Kid White, as his old buddies still called him, was the only one left from the first Montana roundup of 1881.

The old cowpuncher made one more trip to Miles City. After he passed away, on March 6, 1943, at the age of seventy-five, one of his daughters accompanied his body to the former cow town on the Yellowstone for burial, in accordance with his wishes. Charles Wiley led the little procession from the funeral chapel to the Custer County cemetery. Pallbearers were Montana Bill Roberts, Dale Wilder, Harry Reed, Dan Lockie, Sid Vollin, and Casey Barthelmess. All were mounted. That is the way Kid White would have wanted it.

NOTES

An earlier version of this chapter appeared in *Montana*, 17, no. 3 (July, 1967), 60–73.

1. *Rocky Mountain Husbandman* (Great Falls, Mont.), July 2, 1936.
2. Concerning army laundresses during the Indian wars, John R. Sibbald observes: "A private's $13 per month met his own needs rather nicely. Food, shelter, uniform, and transportation were furnished by the government. But the additional demands of a wife and family often made it necessary for an enlisted man's wife and daughters to become laundresses . . . an energetic laundress might add an additional $30 to $40 to the family income. Until 1878 laundresses were carried on the company roster and enjoyed the additional advantages of free rations and transportation" ("Camp Followers All: Army Women of the West," *American West*, 3 [Spring, 1966], 65).
3. Letter from D. J. O'Malley to me, Jan. 1, 1936.
4. *Leader* (Eau Claire, Wis.), July 2, 1941.
5. *Rocky Mountain Husbandman*, Feb. 10, 1938.
6. Undated clipping from the *Nashua* (Mont.) *Independent*, ca. 1934.
7. Undated newspaper clipping from D. J. O'Malley scrapbook.
8. Mari Sandoz, *The Cattlemen* (New York: Hastings House, 1958), p. 325.
9. Like many Ives compositions, this one based on D. J. O'Malley's poem about Charlie Rutledge is something of a musical curiosity. It is included in the Ives folio *Seven Songs for Voice and Piano*, available today from the Associated Music Publishers (New York).
10. Sprague's 1925 recording of "When the Work's All Done This Fall" (Victor 19747) is included in the 1965 RCA Victor Vintage reissue *Authentic Cowboys and Their Western Folksongs* (LPV 522). For the words and tune used by Sprague see chapter 18.
11. John A. Lomax, *Cowboy Songs and Other Frontier Ballads* (New York: Sturgis & Walton Co., 1910), p. 55.
12. Because of this recognition by John A. Lomax, D. J. O'Malley is listed as the author of "Charlie Rutledge," "The Horse Wrangler," and "When the Work's All Done This Fall" in *Granger's Index to Poetry*, 6th ed. (New York: Columbia University Press, 1973), a standard reference work found in most public libraries.
13. Correspondence between J. Frank Dobie and myself, 1934.
14. This is a parody of a religious poem by Urania Locke Bailey (1820–82) which begins

> I want to be an angel,
> And with the angels stand,
> A crown upon my forehead,
> A harp within my hand.

The complete poem appears in Henry T. Coates, ed., *Children's Book of Poetry* (1879; reprinted, Freeport, N.Y.: Books for Libraries, 1973), p. 374, where it is signed with one of Mrs. Bailey's pseudonyms, Sidney Paul Gill.
15. J. Frank Dobie, "Cowboy Songs," *Country Gentleman*, Jan. 10, 1925, p. 9.
16. Undated clipping from the *Nashua* (Mont.) *Independent*, ca. 1934.

8

"The Grass of Uncle Sam"

While researching an article on D. J. O'Malley, Montana cowboy poet,[1] I found in my files a brittle, yellowed copy of the Miles City *Stock Growers' Journal* dated April 4, 1891. This contained the following four stanzas describing cowboy life during the open range days along the Yellowstone in eastern Montana. Untitled, they were signed M.C. and were introduced thus: "Here is the product of a cowboy poet who has developed on our ranges."

Come all you folks from eastern towns,
It's little do you know,
Of the country of the cowboys,
And where your beef steaks grow.
The horses they run wild,
With the mountain sheep and ram,
And the Indians they dwell
On the grass of Uncle Sam.

In the spring-time on the round-up,
We brand the cow and calf,
The pilgrim gets the bucking horse,
You bet that we all laugh.
He throws his arm around the skies,
His legs get in a jam,
And he leaves his impression on
The grass of Uncle Sam.

When we are through our work at night,
And around the campfire lay,
Many stories there are told
And poker games we play.

The cowboy is an honest man,
He fears no trick or sham;
And he sleeps in peace and quietness
On the grass of Uncle Sam.

When the horse thieves get too plentiful,
And more than we can stand,
The vigilant committee
From out the cowboy band,
With Colt's forty-five protectors
With lead their bodies cram,
And we leave them for the coyotes
On the grass of Uncle Sam.

On discovering this rare old copy of Miles City's weekly news-paper, another glance at my files revealed that when I had come into possession of it, in 1934, I had written to D. J. O'Malley, who had contributed many poems to the *Journal* during the nineteen years he worked as a cowpuncher. Recalling that he had signed several of his offerings with fictitious names, I had queried him on this one. He had replied that in this case he was "not guilty." He remembered the verses, however, and said he always had suspected they were com-posed by a self-effacing cowhand named George Matze. George, O'Malley said, worked for a cattleman named M. C. Connors, whose principal brand was MC.

Checking O'Malley's statement about Connors and his brand proved easy. The same issue of the *Journal* carried his advertising—a drawing of a fat steer branded MC and a post office address reading "Spearfish, Dak. Range, Powder River below Deadwood Crossing, Custer Co., M.T." The rest of the story about Matze I had to take on faith.

Whether the rhymester who signed his verses M.C. intended them to be sung is a question. Nevertheless, someone apparently fitted them with a tune and put them into oral circulation, because eight years later, in 1899, a song entitled "The Grass of Uncle Sam" turned up in *Cattle Ranch to College*, a book by Russell Doubleday, a member of New York's well-known publishing family of that name. Oddly, the book was issued by Grosset & Dunlap.

In his narrative, which is subtitled *The True Tale of a Boy's Adventures in the Far West* and has the Dakotas and Montana for its setting, Doubleday has a Montana cowboy sing the stanzas printed below.[2] Note that the original third stanza has been dropped and two new ones added, and that horse thieves now meet their end in a manner somewhat more painful. The two sets of verses are an interest-

In the spring-time on the round-up,
We brand the cow and calf,
The pilgrim gets the bucking horse,
You bet that we all laugh.

This prelude to a bad spill is from a page of ranch-life drawings signed C. M. Russell and J. H. Smith which appeared in *Frank Leslie's Illustrated Newspaper* for May 18, 1889.

ing example of the way a song changed and developed as it was passed around by word of mouth in the days before anyone thought of jingles and ballads about cowboy life as having enough interest, either historically or as entertainment, to be included between the covers of printed songbooks.

Now, peo-ple of the East-ern towns, It's lit-tle that you know A-

bout the West-ern prai-ries, Where the beef you eat does grow; Where the

Git Along, Little Dogies

hors - es they run wild With the moun-tain sheep and ram; And the cow - boy sleeps con - tent - ed On the grass of Un - cle Sam.

Now, people of the Eastern towns,
It's little that you know
About the Western prairies,
Where the beef you eat does grow;
Where the horses they run wild
With the mountain sheep and ram;
And the cow-boy sleeps contented
On the grass of Uncle Sam.

We go out onto the round-up
To brand the sucking calf.
The stranger gets the bucking horse
(You bet then we all laugh).
He flings his arms towards the sky,
His legs get in a jam;
He turns a flying somersault
On the grass of Uncle Sam.

The angry bull takes after us
With blood in both his eyes;
We run, but when his back is turned
He gets a big surprise.
Our ropes jerk out his legs behind
And he goes down *kerslam!*
We drag the fighting out of him
On the grass of Uncle Sam.

The horse-thief comes along at night
To steal our ponies true.
We're always looking out for him,
And sometimes get him, too.
We ask him if he's ready
And when he says "I am,"
The bottoms of his feet they itch
For the grass of Uncle Sam.

And when the round-up's over
To town we go for fun.
The dollars we have hoarded up
Are blown in, every one.
Then broke, we hit the trail for camp,
But we don't care a ———.
Wages are good when the grass is good,
The grass of Uncle Sam.

Russell Doubleday died in 1949. When I became seriously curious about "The Grass of Uncle Sam," I got in touch with his widow and inquired about his western experiences. Her reply contained the surprising statement that her husband's book had been written without his ever having been in the West. Mrs. Doubleday added: "He met a young lawyer named Tom McKee, whose story is told in *Cattle Ranch to College*. They spent a great amount of time together, and Tom checked up on everything in the book. They were both about twenty-four or twenty-five years old at the time."[3]

I have never heard of "The Grass of Uncle Sam" being put on a phonograph record, and I have seen only one other printed version—in *Songs of the Open Range*, compiled by Miss Ina Sires, a Dallas schoolteacher, and published in 1928 by C. C. Birchard & Company. Miss Sires, who now lives in Hollywood, California, once spent a summer on a ranch near Malta, Montana, where she presumably picked up the song. Her rendering is almost identical with Doubleday's except that the opening stanza is missing and there is no resemblance whatever between the two tunes.[4]

NOTES

An earlier version of this chapter appeared in *Western Folklore*, 28 (Oct., 1969), 267–71.

1. John I. White, "A Montana Cowboy Poet," *Journal of American Folklore*, 80 (Apr.-June, 1967), 113–29.
2. Russell Doubleday, *Cattle Ranch to College: The True Tale of a Boy's Adventures in the Far West* (New York: Grosset & Dunlap, 1899), pp. 269, 270, 271. The tune given above is from Ina Sires, *Songs of the Open Range* (Boston: C. C. Birchard and Co., 1928), pp. 30–31. Doubleday's tune is reproduced in my *Western Folklore* article.
3. Letter from Janet M. Doubleday to me, Mar. 14, 1967.
4. *Western Folklore*, 29 (July, 1970), 196–98, published a variant of "The Grass of Uncle Sam" supplied by Austin E. Fife, a ten-stanza text from the Robert W. Gordon manuscript collection at the Library of Congress. Dr. Fife reports that it was sent to Gordon by Bradford Shaw, "who says it was sung to the tune of 'Limerick Town.' "

9

And That's How
a "Folksong" Was Born

Here's an ugly brute from the cattle chute,
Press along to the Big Corral.
The big galoot's got a bottle in his boot,
Press along to the Big Corral.

Press along, cowboy, press along,
Press along with a cowboy yell.
Press along with a noise, big noise,
Press along to the Big Corral.

Sounds like a nonsense song? You are so right! It *was* nonsense during Prohibition days in 1922 when the late Romaine Lowdermilk and two of his neighbors mounted the stage at a local talent show in Wickenburg, Arizona, and sang these words plus additional stanzas lampooning themselves and other citizens of the little town on the Hassayampa that hadn't yet thought of calling itself "Dude Ranch Capital of the World." Nonsense then, perhaps, but in the half-century that has elapsed since then a great many people have taken "The Big Corral" dead seriously.

Romaine borrowed the tune of the gospel hymn "Press Along to Glory Land," written in 1911 by James Rowe and Emmett S. Dean, and the boys made up their own verses to fit whatever local situation they thought would get a laugh. It was all very funny. After the show the audience congratulated the performers on their inventiveness, never dreaming they had been present at the birth of a western American "folksong." Then everybody promptly forgot about "The Big Corral." Everybody, that is, except Romaine.

Two years later, by an unexplainable stroke of luck, I visited

This photograph of Romaine Lowdermilk
(1890–1970) was taken in March, 1941.

Romaine Lowdermilk on his small cattle ranch, Kay-El-Bar, at Wickenburg. Romaine "flogged a gee-tar," and we sat around and sang. I learned many of his songs; I am sure he learned many of mine. One day he gave out with "The Big Corral," an incongruous mixture of ideas seemingly concerning a ranch cook and heaven. At the time I had no idea where it originated, but I tucked it away in my memory and on my way back home was humming:

> This ugly gink is a half-breed Chink,
> Press along to the Big Corral.
> He makes his clink in the kitchen sink,
> Press along to the Big Corral.

A few years later I was "flogging a gee-tar" myself, backed up by a male quartet, while singing western ballads from a New York radio station. With a little help from me, a station pianist turned out a bang-up arrangement of "The Big Corral" that we rendered on the slightest excuse.

With cowboy songs enjoying popularity through the far-reaching effects of radio, the logical follow-up was to publish some of those I had

This 1929 cartoon by J. R. Williams supplied a stanza for the nonsense song "The Big Corral." Reprinted by permission of Newspaper Enterprise Association.

collected in the West, most of them at the Kay-El-Bar in Wickenburg. "The Big Corral" naturally was among these. Unable to recall all of Romaine's words, I made up a few lines myself and even borrowed two from an "Out Our Way" cowboy cartoon by J. R. Williams, as follows:

> The wrangler's out a-combin' the hills,
> Press along to the Big Corral.
> So jump in yore britches and grease up yore gills,
> Press along to the Big Corral.

My song folio *The Lonesome Cowboy: Songs of the Plains and Hills*, compiled with George Shackley, was published in 1929. Except for a few pieces with words by established western poets such as E. A. Brininstool and James Barton Adams, the songs included were considered "traditional," and nobody else got any credit, not even Romaine. Here is "The Big Corral" as it appeared in *The Lonesome Cowboy*.

Git Along, Little Dogies

This ugly brute from the cattle chute,
Press along to the Big Corral.
He should be branded on the snoot,
Press along to the Big Corral.

Press along, cowboy, press along,
Press along with a cowboy yell,
Press along with a noise, big noise,
Press along to the Big Corral.

This ugly gink is a half-breed chink,
Press along to the Big Corral.
He makes his bread in the kitchen sink,
Press along to the Big Corral.

The chuck we get ain't fit to eat,
Press along to the Big Corral.
There's rocks in the beans and sand in the meat,
Press along to the Big Corral.

Early in the mornin', 'bout half past four,
Press along to the Big Corral.
You hear him open his face to roar,
Press along to the Big Corral.

The wrangler's out a-combin' the hills,
Press along to the Big Corral.
So jump in yore britches and grease up yore gills,
Press along to the Big Corral.[1]

Shortly after, cowboy song folios began appearing by the dozens, and mine soon disappeared—but not before other singers had spotted "The Big Corral" with its nonsensical words, its borrowed hymn tune, and its bang-up male quartet arrangement. It soon was on records, being sung in schools and summer camps and attracting the attention of folksong collectors. I have seen at least twenty-five books, eight of them hard-cover publications chiefly for school use, that include this supposedly traditional cowboy song. There must be others. Looking back, I realize that if "The Big Corral" had had Romaine Lowder-milk's name on it when it first appeared in print, publishers would have avoided it for fear of copyright infringement and it probably would have died long ago.

Some of the editorial comments in books containing "The Big Corral" supplied a few hearty chuckles for Romaine and me. In 1951, the eminent musicologist Charles Haywood paid the song an unusual compliment in his monumental work *A Bibliography of North American Folklore and Folksong*. Under published collections of cowboy songs he lists George F. Briegel's *Home on the Range: Cowboy Song Book*, issued in 1936, and comments: "Twenty-five Cowboy tunes. Out of this group only five are authentic folk tunes, the rest are composed imitations. The five are: Home on the Range; The Big Rock Candy Mountain; Goodbye Old Paint; The Big Corral, and Echo Canyon (Mormon Railroad Song)."[2]

Kansas-born singer Frank Luther, who recorded "The Big Corral" in 1950 on Decca DL 5053, also put it in his 1942 book, *Americans and Their Songs*, with this introduction: "Into the railroad corrals the cowboys drove their longhorns with many a yip and shout. They drove them up the chutes and into the cattle cars, a scene to live long in memory; a scene to live longer in a noisy, driving song called The Big Corral."[3]

Noted composer Elie Siegmeister, in his book *Work and Sing: A Collection of the Songs That Built America,* introduced "The Big Corral" this way: "As he rounds up his steers and drives them into the big corral or cowpen, the cattle man does not usually think of the glories of the great outdoors. In this song we hear him bellowing forth his opinion of 'that chuck (food) wagon brute'—the cook, whose duty it is not only to feed the cowboys, but also to get them up at four-thirty a.m."[4] Composer Siegmeister thought enough of "The Big Corral" to include it in a second book, *Singing down the Road*, arranged for male voices and published principally for school use by Ginn & Company in 1947.

Even though its origin has been nailed down tight, who is to say that "The Big Corral" is not a folksong? In its anonymous state it has been around since 1929 and by most definitions it probably qualifies. Almost every printed version differs from the others. Nearly every modern troubadour who has touched it has changed the words and music to suit his own notion of a cowboy song or to fit his own style of singing. Certainly the following, published in 1944 in a folio by Sterling Sherwin called *Singing in the Saddle*, has little resemblance to Lowdermilk's original.

> The ugly baboon is a half-breed loon,
> Press along to the Big Corral.
> He makes his biscuits in a goboon,
> Press along to the Big Corral.[5]

During his long career as a professional cowboy singer and entertainer, Romaine Lowdermilk composed a number of other songs, several of which were published with his name attached. Among these was "Back to Old Montana," which in 1935 was included in the M. M. Cole folio *100 WLS Barn Dance Favorites*, and in 1940 was recorded by RCA Victor cowgirl singer Patsy Montana.[6] The song actually began life as "Back to Arizona," in which a cowboy who went east was hit by a bad spell of homesickness and sang this chorus:

> I'm going back to Arizona,
> That's where I want to be.

I've got a gal in Arizona
I'd like mighty well to see.
I've got a cow in Arizona
With a calf I'd like to brand,
I've got a hoss in Arizona
Running with a mustang band.
I'm going back to Arizona
And round them up some day,
And whoop and yell in the big corral,
Come a ti yi yippy yippy yea.

In reminiscing about the above, Romaine had this to say: "Patsy Montana liked it and wanted to sing it on her road appearances, so I just called it 'Back to Old Montana' and she recorded it for Victor and it was on the juke boxes for quite a spell. You can sing it 'Back to California,' or Oklahoma or Wyoming—or any damn place you want to go back to. So I figured it was an all-around western. I got paid for it by WLS, so didn't really care where the singer went back to."[7]

Other published compositions by Romaine were "Mr. Cowboy Goes to Town," a yodeling song included in *Patsy Montana's America's No. 1 Cowgirl Song Folio*, and "The Rodeo Parade," a march-time number published in a folio called *Stuart Hamblen and His Lucky Stars*.

While these three numbers with Romaine's brand on them earned a little fame and money for their writer, they had their day. But that maverick "The Big Corral," which never made a nickel for him nor earned him one bit of credit until this account of its career first appeared in print, in the *Arizona Republic* for August 13, 1967, still is very much in evidence in classrooms and school libraries. It pays to get put between hard covers; it helps with both status and longevity.

As for recordings, a Chicago disc-collecting and researching friend of mine, Harlan Daniel, tells me Decca has issued at least five with "The Big Corral," that it was recorded by Alan Mills in 1953 (*More Songs to Grow On*, Folkways FP 709) and Rex Trailer in 1965 (*Country and Western*, Crown 5158 [monaural], 186 [stereo]). In 1956 it was the lead song on *Favorite Cowboy Songs* by the Sons of the Pioneers (RCA Victor LPM 1130). The oldest disc is a 78 rpm single made in 1932 by Glen Rice and His Beverly Hillbillies (Brunswick 598). The piece appears on a handful of other records. For some reason, Romaine himself never made any commercial recordings of the songs he loved to sing. He just seemed to shun the idea.

Before selling out at Wickenburg in 1927, Romaine operated his Kay-El-Bar for a short time as a dude ranch. Then he built a ranch at

Romaine Lowdermilk and the Arizona Wranglers photographed at the Arizona Biltmore Hotel during the winter of 1929–30. *Left to right:* Charles Hunter, J. E. Patterson, Lowdermilk, Edward V. Price (in tuxedo), Laverne Costello, and Charles English. Price was a clothing merchant who hoped to arrange a national radio hook-up for merchandising his line of men's furnishings. His advertising ideas were ahead of the broadcasting equipment then available. Later the musicians, except for Lowdermilk, went to station KNX, Hollywood, where the group added several members and enjoyed a tremendous success for about five years.

Judging by the mournful expression on the faces of the three musical notes, Romaine Lowdermilk is giving out with a sad one, such as "Blood on the Saddle" or "Billy the Kid." The cartoon was drawn in 1950 to illustrate an *Arizona Republic* feature story on the cowboy entertainer. The artist, Frank King, has generously consented to its reproduction.

Rimrock that he eventually sold to the Eaton brothers, pioneer Wyoming dude ranchers. In the late 1920s he did a two-year stint as an entertainer at the Arizona Biltmore. Later he owned several other dude ranches, where his renderings of "Blood on the Saddle," "The Strawberry Roan," "Great Grandad," and "The Santa Fe Trail" were as much an attraction for easterners as the Arizona scenery and sunshine.

Romaine's career as a singer, minus his connection with "The Big Corral," is detailed in *Folksingers and Folksongs in America* by the late Ray M. Lawless, a professor at Metropolitan Junior College, Kansas City, Missouri. The account ends with these characteristic comments by Lowdermilk himself:

> I was just lucky to be born early enough to get acquainted with some of the cowboys who had worked the ranges through the 70's and 80's, to see occasional actual longhorns on open range. I saw big roundups and drives; saw the old backyard cowboy reunion commercialized into the modern rodeo; saw bands of wild horses on mountain and plain and the gradual change from the genuine Spanish mustang through the bronco era to fine quarter-horses. Have seen altered brands, cow thieves, blackleg, ticks, pink-eye, screw worms, bad men in high places and good men

on the dodge, stampedes, range arguments, water troubles, storms, droughts, and lots of bright sunshine and fair weather when

> "Everything's lovely and nothin' is wrong,
> And I'm just lazy-like, lopin' along."[8]

Music was not the only extracurricular activity filling the pages of ex-cowboy Romaine Lowdermilk's memory book when he passed away at Phoenix in June of 1970, just a few days after reaching the eighty mark. Many years ago while ranching on the Hassayampa he had developed a talent for writing, an extremely handy side business for anyone attempting to raise beef on the rocky, cactus-studded desert at Wickenburg. Two of his best yarns, both originally printed in *Adventure Magazine*, have been preserved in anthologies. "The Passing of Pete Davila," a touching story of an outlaw who redeemed himself in a gold camp owned by an understanding Irishman, can be found in *Arizona Literature*, edited by Mary G. Boyer. "The Spirit of His Youth," in which a septuagenarian ranch cook rises to an emergency, is in Oren Arnold's *Roundup of Western Literature: An Anthology for Young Readers*.[9]

Romaine also got to Hollywood for a brief stay when one of his literary efforts, "Tucker's Top Hand," a novelette in *Short Stories Magazine*, was filmed, in the silent screen days. Neal Hart was the leading man. "The less said about my horse opera the better," was Lowdermilk's wry comment some forty years later. "It came out just like a million others."[10]

NOTES

An earlier version of this chapter appeared in the *Arizona Republic* (Phoenix) Sunday supplement, August 13, 1967.

1. John White and George Shackley, *The Lonesome Cowboy: Songs of the Plains and Hills* (New York: Al Piantadosi, 1929), pp. 43–45.
2. Charles Haywood, *A Bibliography of North American Folklore and Folksong* (New York: Greenberg, 1951), p. 619. This information remained unchanged in the second, revised edition (New York: Dover Publications, 1961), vol. 1, p. 619.
3. Frank Luther, *Americans and Their Songs* (New York and London: Harper & Brothers, 1942), p. 195.
4. Elie Siegmeister, *Work and Sing: A Collection of the Songs That Built America* (New York: William R. Scott, 1944), p. 29.
5. Sterling Sherwin, *Singing in the Saddle* (Boston: Boston Music Co., 1944).
6. The title in the folio is "Goin' Back to Old Montana."
7. Letter from Romaine H. Lowdermilk to me, Feb. 8, 1967. The stanza of "Back to Arizona" is given as Romaine sang it.
8. Ray M. Lawless, *Folksingers and Folksongs in America* (New York: Duell, Sloan and Pearce, 1960), p. 147.
9. Mary G. Boyer, ed., *Arizona Literature* (Glendale, Calif.: Arthur H. Clark Co., 1934), pp. 54–73; Oren Arnold, *Roundup of Western Literature: An Anthology for Young Readers* (Dallas: Banks, Upshaw and Co., 1949), pp. 130–52.
10. Letter from Romaine H. Lowdermilk to me, Feb. 8, 1967.

10

Gail Gardner, Cowboy "Poet Lariat"

In the summer of 1924 at a picnic near the Tonto ranger station west of Prescott, Arizona, I heard a young fellow recite a poem he had written, titled "The Sierry Petes," about tying knots in the devil's tail. He was Gail I. Gardner, and the verses I heard have since become the basis for one of the best known of all genuine cowboy songs produced since the turn of the century.

> Away up high in the Sierry Petes,[1]
> Where the yeller pines grows tall,
> Ole Sandy Bob an' Buster Jig,
> Had a rodeer camp[2] last fall.
>
> Oh, they taken their hosses and runnin' irons[3]
> And mabbe a dawg or two,
> An' they 'lowed they'd brand all the long-yered calves,
> That come within their view.
>
> And any old dogie that flapped long yeres,
> An' didn't bush up[4] by day,
> Got his long yeres whittled an' his old hide scortched,
> In a most artistic way.
>
> Now one fine day ole Sandy Bob,
> He throwed his seago[5] down,
> "I'm sick of the smell of burnin' hair,
> And I 'lows I'm a-goin' to town."
>
> So they saddles up an' hits 'em a lope,
> Fer it warn't no sight of a ride,
> And them was the days when a Buckeroo
> Could ile up his inside.

Oh, they starts her in at the Kaintucky Bar,
At the head of Whisky Row,
And they winds up down by the Depot House,
Some forty drinks below.

They then sets up[6] and turns around,
And goes her the other way,
An' to tell you the Gawd-forsaken truth,
Them boys got stewed that day.

As they was a-ridin' back to camp,
A-packin' a pretty good load,
Who should they meet but the Devil himself,
A-prancin' down the road.

Sez he, "You ornery cowboy skunks,
You'd better hunt yer holes,
Fer I've come up from Hell's Rim Rock,
To gather in yer souls."

Sez Sandy Bob, "Old Devil be damned,
We boys is kinda tight,
But you ain't a-goin' to gather no cowboy souls,
'Thout you has some kind of a fight."

So Sandy Bob punched a hole in his rope,
And he swang her straight and true,
He lapped it on to the Devil's horns,
An' he taken his dallies[7] too.

Now Buster Jig was a riata man,
With his gut-line[8] coiled up neat,
So he shaken her out an' he built him a loop,
An' he lassed the Devil's hind feet.

Oh, they stretched him out an' they tailed him down,[9]
While the irons was a-gettin' hot,
They cropped and swaller-forked[10] his yeres,
Then they branded him up a lot.

They pruned him up with a de-hornin' saw,
An' they knotted his tail fer a joke,
They then rid off and left him there,
Necked[11] to a Black-Jack oak.

If you're ever up high in the Sierry Petes,
An' you hear one Hell of a wail,
You'll know it's that Devil a-bellerin' around,
About them knots in his tail.[12]

But because Gardner's tall tale about the unusual antics of two inebriated Arizona cowpokes caught the fancy of cowboy singers

This spoof of an Arizona dude-ranching situation drawn by J. R. Williams in 1933 contains a stanza from the famous song "The Sierry Petes" written by the artist's neighbor, Gail I. Gardner. For years Williams, a former cowpuncher, mule skinner, and cavalryman, collected material for his popular "Out Our Way" cartoon series on annual visits to the Southwest. In the early 1930s he succumbed completely to the lure of Arizona and acquired his own ranch in a wild region along Walnut Creek northwest of Prescott. Reprinted by permission of Newspaper Enterprise Association.

everywhere, it soon moved into the traditional ballad category and beyond the control of its author. As a result, it has appeared in at least a dozen printed song collections and can be heard on about as many discs, in both cases usually without a by-your-leave to the originator, although in recent years he has been able to collect a few modest royalties.[13]

Gardner, who lives at Prescott in the house where he was born in 1892, has become more or less resigned to having others appropriate his work. His main gripe is that people don't sing the song the way he wrote it. When a ballad is passed around verbally from one singer to another, it often gets changed here and there, particularly when it contains words or phrases whose meanings are not always readily apparent. An examination of Gardner's verses reveals several that would be obscure to anybody but a northern Arizona cowboy of the old school. For instance, there is an allusion to a cowpunching practice once peculiar to the mountainous Prescott region. To quote the author: "The part about tying the devil up to a black jack oak is lost on all the flat country buckaroos, because in this country *only* do they handle outlaw cattle by tying them to trees, leaving them a night or so, and then leading them in. No reflection on other cowboys; they have no necessity for that kind of work and they never heard of it. Neither do they have black jack oaks, something for which they may be thankful."[14]

Gardner's title, too, has given singers plenty of trouble. He called his poem "The Sierry Petes" and uses the same expression in the first line. This, he says, is the local nickname for the Sierra Prieta, a mountain range southwest of Prescott. In various printed and recorded versions this often comes out as Siren Peaks or Siree Peaks.

The "Whisky Row" mentioned in the sixth stanza of the poem is Montezuma Street, Prescott, which runs along one side of the Yavapai County courthouse. Way back before Prohibition, among the saloons there really was a Kentucky Bar at one end, and on North Cortez Street, next to the railroad station, a saloon called the Depot House.

While Gardner never got around to copyrighting his poem until 1935, it actually was published as far back as 1929, with credit to the author, in a pamphlet put together by George German, a South Dakotan. The latter worked for a while in Arizona, then returned home to Yankton and published a small collection called *Cowboy Campfire Ballads*. This contained only the words of the songs, no tunes. While Gardner was appreciative of the acknowledgment, he regrets that German didn't come to him for the original instead of picking up a garbled version from a dude ranch entertainer.

In a pamphlet of his own, first issued in December, 1935, and reprinted several times since, Gardner explains the origin of his salty bit of range poetry:

> . . . one time I was camped with the late Bob Heckle at the old Bill Dearing Ranch in the Sierra Prieta (Sierry Petes) mountains west of Prescott. One day we came into town for a little "whizzer," and on the way back to camp, one of us remarked that the devil got cowboys for doing what we had been doing. That was the germ of an idea that came to life on a Santa Fe train in 1917 when I was headed back to Washington,

As a personal favor to his friend and neighbor Gail
Gardner, cartoonist-rancher J. R. Williams drew this
cover for Gail's modest booklet of poems, *Orejana
Bull for Cowboys Only*, first issued in 1935. *Orejana*,
Gail explains, refers to an animal old enough to leave
its mother but unbranded and not ear-marked—in
other words, a maverick.

D.C., to get into military service. The gentle, broad-beamed cattle in
the fields of Kansas were so different from the stock Bob and I had been
working that I was inspired to write some verses about some drunken
cowboys handling the devil the same way they handled wild cattle.[15]

Gardner mailed the verses back to his sister in Prescott. After the
war he showed them to a friend, Bill Simon, who composed a simple
tune and began singing them. Other Arizonans picked up the song
and it soon spread over the West. Here is the tune as I have been
singing it for forty-odd years:

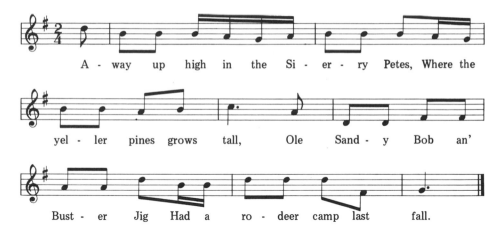

A - way   up   high   in   the   Si - er - ry   Petes,   Where the

yel - ler   pines   grows   tall,   Ole   Sand - y   Bob   an'

Bust - er   Jig   Had   a   ro - deer   camp   last   fall.

Gardner says he himself sang "The Sierry Petes" the first time for the cowboys attending one of a series of neighborhood rodeos staged on the Z-Triangle Ranch near Wagoner owned by James Minotto. The boys like it. Liked it so much that for each of the next few years Gardner had to come up with a new one. Those that he feels have made the best songs are "The Moonshine Steer" and "The Dude Wrangler." The former, which can be sung to the tune of "Roving Gambler," also deals with two cowboys on a binge. They discover a moonshine still and, after quenching their own thirst, pour a quart of corn down the throat of a wild steer, with disastrous results. The final stanza reads:

> This story has a moral,
> And you will find it here.
> If you ever have any moonshine,
> Don't waste none on no steer.[16]

"The Dude Wrangler," a long, rambling, tongue-in-cheek ballad that I have heard sung well by veteran entertainer Romaine H. Lowdermilk of Phoenix and my brother, rancher Bob White of Wickenburg, was written at a time when cow work was scarce for Arizona cowboys and, to quote Gardner, "a lot of them had to go to work as dude wranglers at Castle Hot Springs." In the song the narrator tells a sorrowful tale about an old partner of his, a hard-bitten cowhand who never in his life had owned any clothes other than Levi's. One day when they meet he is dressed in a different fashion:

> He had his boots outside his britches;
> They was made of leather green and red.
> His shirt was of a dozen colors,
> Loud enough to wake the dead.

Gail I. Gardner photographed in the early 1920s at the Devil's Gate roundup grounds, Skull Valley, Arizona. His hat—small, flat-brimmed, and with a dented crown—was typical, he says, of those then worn by Yavapai County cowpunchers. The leather chaps and the tapaderos over the stirrups both afforded the rider protection from the thorny brush so abundant in the Southwest. The horse, bought by Gardner from another rancher, is branded Bar Circle A.

> Around his neck he had a 'kerchief,
> Knotted through a silver ring;
> I swear to Gawd he had a wrist watch,
> Who ever heard of such a thing?

There is much more, including a description of the old-timer shepherding lady riders, then the climax:

So I drawed my gun and throwed it on him,
I had to turn my face away.
I shot him squarely through the middle,
And where he fell I left him lay.

I shorely hated for to do it,
For things that's done you cain't recall,
But when a cowboy turns dude wrangler,
He ain't no good no more at all.[17]

Previous to his brief World War I service, in the fledgling Air Corps, Gardner had attended Dartmouth College, worked in his father's pioneer general store in Prescott, and run a small cow outfit at Skull Valley in partnership with Van Dickson. Later he bought out his partner and operated on his own. From 1936 to 1957 he was Prescott's postmaster. But he held on to his little ranch until 1960. Looking back, he has this to say: "Hard and lean as they were, I believe I had more fun in the cowboy years than at any other time. Sometimes even now, I think I would like to get out and 'bust a loop at one' (arthritis and bum eyesight permitting), but when I think of the years it forgot to rain, or some of the hard winters with six inches of snow on the oak brush, I am fairly content to settle down in the old arm chair and watch the sky stay up."[18]

NOTES

An earlier version of this chapter appeared in the *Arizona Republic* (Phoenix) Sunday supplement, May 7, 1967.

1. *Sierry Petes*—local nickname for a mountain range, the Sierra Prieta, southwest of Prescott, Arizona.
2. *Rodeer camp*—roundup camp, from the Spanish verb *rodear*, meaning "to surround."
3. *Runnin' irons*—curved strips of iron with which one could burn *any* brand on an animal's hide. The opposite is the stamp iron, which makes only one design.
4. *Bush up*—hide in the bushes.
5. *Seago*—a "lass rope" made of fiber something like maguey. Says Gardner: "No Yavapai County cowboy would ever say 'lasso.' A steer breaks out and somebody yells 'lass him.' The cowboy's catch rope is his 'lass rope' or just his 'rope' " (letter from Gail Gardner to me, Sept. 23, 1966).
6. *Sets up*—pull up their horses when going at a fast clip.
7. *Taken his dallies*—snubbed the end of his rope around the saddle horn, from the Spanish *dar la vuelta*, meaning "to take a turn."
8. *Riata, gut-line*—a "lass rope" made of braided rawhide.
9. *Tailed him down*—"In roping big cattle," Gardner says, "one cowboy 'heads' (ropes by the head or horns) and the other 'heels' (ropes the animal by one or both hind feet). A big, strong animal will sometimes brace both front feet wide apart and is stretched out but is not down, so one cowboy, usually the 'header,' after making sure his rope is secured to the saddle horn, gets off his horse, grabs the critter by the tail, and gives a heavy yank sideways, which lays him on his side" (letter from Gardner to me, July 20, 1973).
10. *Swaller-forked*—notched each ear so that it resembled the forked tail of a swallow—just one of the many ways of earmarking a calf. On earmarking, Gardner contributes the following: "A

brand is really the ultimate verification of an earmark and what legally indicates the ownership of the animal. When you approach a bunch of cattle, they put up their ears and you identify ownership at a glance. A brand may be on one side or the other—hips, ribs, or shoulder—and it may have long hair over it in winter. So when cutting cattle from a milling herd you have to go by the earmarks" (letter from Gardner to me, Sept. 23, 1966).

11. *Necked*—tied by the neck.

12. Gail I. Gardner, *Orejana Bull for Cowboys Only*, 4th printing (Phoenix: Messenger Printing Co., 1965), pp. 9–10.

13. Gail Gardner recorded "The Sierry Petes" himself for an LP issued in 1971 by the Arizona Friends of Folklore at Northern Arizona University (Flagstaff). The disc, titled *Cowboy Songs* (AFF 33–1), also includes his renderings of two other Gardner poems that have been set to music, "The Moonshine Steer" and "The Cowman's Troubles." All three are sung without accompaniment.

14. Letter from Gardner to me, Feb. 23, 1932.

15. Gardner, *Orejana Bull*, [p. 6].

16. Ibid., p. 12.

17. Ibid., pp. 15, 16.

18. Ibid., [p. 7].

11

Badger Clark,
Poet of Yesterday's West

Arizona's abundant sunshine and superb scenery probably have inspired enough poetry to paper at least one wall of the Grand Canyon. However, few poets enamored of the desert have equaled the record of Badger Clark, a Methodist minister's son who arrived from the Black Hills of South Dakota in 1906 at the age of twenty-three, seeking health, spent four years on a cow ranch near Tombstone, and while there penned enough good solid verses on cowboy life and the great outdoors to fill a substantial book.

First issued in 1915, Clark's notable collection *Sun and Saddle Leather* went through many editions with Boston publishers, the last in 1942. The book has been kept in print, thanks to the Westerners Foundation, which brought out a new edition in 1962.[1]

Among Badger Clark's poems are two that have been turned into widely circulated songs, not by professional tunesmiths from Tin Pan Alley but by Arizona cowboys. One of these, called "The Glory Trail" by its author and "High-Chin Bob" by many who have sung it, has the Mogollon Rim northeast of Phoenix as its setting. In this dramatic narrative—one that has found its way into numerous poetry anthologies as well as becoming a song—an over-confident cowhand ropes a mountain lion in the expectation of dragging it to death. The poem begins on this optimistic note:

> 'Way high up the Mogollons,
> Among the mountain tops,
> A lion cleaned a yearlin's bones
> And licked his thankful chops,
> When on the picture who should ride,

A studio portrait of Badger Clark in his
thirties after returning from Arizona to
South Dakota, his boyhood home. Courtesy
of Badger Clark Memorial Center, Dakota
Wesleyan University.

A-trippin' down a slope,
But High-Chin Bob, with sinful pride
And mav'rick hungry rope.

"Oh, glory be to me," says he,
"And fame's unfadin' flowers!
All meddlin' hands are far away;
I ride my good top-hawse today
And I'm top-rope of the Lazy J—
Hi! kitty cat, you're ours!"

High-Chin Bob dropped a loop on his lion, to be sure, but discovered
to his sorrow that the cougar had more staying power than anticipated.

Three suns had rode their circle home
Beyond the desert's rim,
And turned their star-herds loose to roam
The ranges high and dim;
Yet up and down and 'round and 'cross
Bob pounded, weak and wan,
For pride still glued him to his hawse
And glory drove him on.

"Oh, glory be to me," sighs he.
"He kain't be drug to death,
But now I know beyond a doubt
Them heroes I have read about
Was only fools that stuck it out
To end of mortal breath."

It is said that High-Chin Bob's ghost still is riding, riding a pale horse, with a shadowy mountain lion trailing behind. Here is the final stanza:

'Way high up the Mogollons
A prospect man did swear
That moon dreams melted down his bones
And hoisted up his hair:
A ribby cow-hawse thundered by,
A lion trailed along,
A rider ga'nt but chin on high,
Yelled out a crazy song.

"Oh, glory be to me!" cries he,
"And to my noble noose!
Oh, stranger, tell my pards below
I took a rampin' dream in tow,
And if I never lay him low,
I'll never turn him loose!"[2]

Artist Joe Beeler of Sedona and editor Joseph Stacey graciously consented to the use of this drawing of Badger Clark's mythical hero High-Chin Bob, orginally reproduced in *Arizona Highways* for February, 1969.

Bill Simon tuning up at the bunkhouse door in 1921, when he was a wagon boss for the King Brothers, an outfit that at one time ran ten thousand head of cattle in Yavapai and Coconino counties. Bill's career included a long stretch of entertaining on the rodeo circuit with a husband-and-wife comedy act. Today, past eighty, he teaches riding at Prescott. In the spring of 1971 Bill and his neighbor Gail Gardner starred in a twenty-nine-minute documentary, *The Last Wagon*, directed by folksinger Katie Lee and filmed by Harry Atwood of the University of Arizona Radio-TV Bureau.

More polished and better suited for musical rendition is Clark's Arizona poem "A Border Affair," first published in the *Pacific Monthly* for June, 1907 (the version given below). "A Border Affair" naturally was included in the book *Sun and Saddle Leather*. Back in 1925 cowboy singer Bill Simon of Prescott, the first to fit a tune to Gail Gardner's famous yarn about tying knots in the devil's tail, spotted Clark's poetic love story and concluded it should make a good song. Bill thereupon composed an engaging melody, and before long, dude ranch entertainers and radio performers throughout the Southwest were singing:

Span - ish is the lov - in' tongue, Soft as mu - sic, light__ as spray; 'Twas a girl I learnt it from Liv - in' down So - no - ra way. I dont look much like a lov - er, Yet I say her love - words o - ver Of - ten, when I'm all a - lone — "*Mi a - mor, mi co - ra - zón!*"

Spanish is the lovin' tongue,
Soft as music, light as spray;
'T was a girl I learnt it from
Livin' down Sonora way.
I dont look much like a lover,
Yet I say her love-words over
Often, when I'm all alone—
"*Mi amor, mi corazón.*"

Nights when she knew where I'd ride
She would listen for my spurs,
Throw the big door open wide,
Raise them laughin' eyes of hers,
And my heart would nigh stop beatin'
When I'd hear her tender greetin'
Whispered soft for me alone—
"Mi amor! mi corazón!"

Moonlight in the patio,
Old Señora noddin' near,
Me and Juana talkin' low
So the "madre" couldn't hear—
How those hours would go a-flying',
And too soon I'd hear her sighin',
In her little sorry-tone—
"Adiós, mi corazón."

But one time I had to fly
For a foolish gamblin' fight,
And we said a swift good-bye
On that black, unlucky night.
When I'd loosed her arms from clingin',
With her words the hoofs kept ringin',
As I galloped north alone—
"Adiós, mi corazón."

Never seen her since that night;
I kaint cross the Line, you know.
She was Mex. and I was white;[3]
Like as not it's better so.
Yet I've always sort of missed her
Since that last, wild night I kissed her,
Left her heart and lost my own—
"Adiós, mi corazón."

Says Bill Simon, who until recently never received any credit in print for his contribution to the music of the West: "I can neither read nor write music. I just somehow worked out 'Spanish Is the Lovin' Tongue' as I rode the range, trying to fit the words in a melody I was striving for. After I got it to the point where it suited me, I started singing it around the campfires and it seemed to catch on. One night Dorothy Youmans (sister of composer Vincent Youmans) heard me sing it and was quite taken with it. Later she wrote out the music for me and played it on the piano down at Castle Hot Springs while I sang. Well, it sure sounded good."[4]

I first heard the song in Wickenburg, in 1933. Completely unaware

Badger Clark finds time for relaxation at the Cross I Quarter Circle Ranch near Tombstone, Arizona, where he spent four years—probably the happiest of his life—and wrote his best-known poems. Courtesy of Badger Clark Memorial Center, Dakota Wesleyan University.

of the tune's origin, I wrote it out as it appears above and sent it to Badger Clark with a request for permission to use it on a network radio program. The poet was pleasantly surprised to learn that another of his many works had been set to music. Until then he had heard only of "High-Chin Bob" having been given this special honor. Bill Simon recorded his own arrangement of "Spanish Is the Lovin' Tongue" for an LP issued in 1972 by the Arizona Friends of Folklore at Northern Arizona University (Flagstaff), *Cowboy Songs*, 2 (AFF 33–2). His tune differs in many respects from the one I wrote down in 1933.

"In Arizony" was the title of Badger Clark's first published poem. He wrote it a few months after settling down on the Cross I Quarter Circle Ranch some fifteen miles out of Tombstone. When writing home to his stepmother, the twenty-three-year-old apprentice cowboy expressed his feeling of contentment with his new life by enclosing the composition which begins:

> There is some that like the city—
> Grass that's curried smooth and green,

Theaytres and stranglin' collars,
Wagons run by gasoline—
But for me it's hawse and saddle
Every day without a change,
And a desert sun a-blazin'
On a hundred miles of range.
 Just a-ridin', a-ridin'—
 Desert ripplin' in the sun,
 Mountains blue along the skyline—
 I don't envy anyone
 When I'm ridin'.[5]

The fledgling poet's proud stepmother promptly sent the verses to the *Pacific Monthly*, a leading western magazine of that time. The editor just as promptly sent the surprised young man a check for ten dollars and ran "In Arizony" in the August, 1906, issue. Later Clark placed this poem first in the group selected for *Sun and Saddle Leather*, at the same time changing its title to "Ridin'."

Clark's Arizona word-pictures obviously were considered a find by the magazine's editor. In the September, 1906, issue he ran a second poem, "A Bad Half Hour." The October issue had two—"The Round-up" and "Bacon." Starting with March, 1907, the *Pacific Monthly* carried a Clark poem every month for sixteen months, or through June, 1908. July, 1908, had a Clark short story titled "The Man Kind." August had another poem, "Goodbye Old Forty-Five," which, like "The Roundup" mentioned above, failed to make the grade when the contents of *Sun and Saddle Leather* were chosen. In the magazine all of these were signed Charles B. Clark, Jr. It was not until his work began appearing in book form that the poet began calling himself by his middle name.

In 1910 Clark left Arizona and returned to the Black Hills, where he spent the remainder of his life. For nearly twenty years prior to his death in 1957 at the age of seventy-four, he had the honor of being South Dakota's poet laureate. He remained a bachelor all his days. His wants, which were few, were supplied by fees from speaking engagements, largely confined to South Dakota, and meager royalties from his writings. These included a book of prose called *Spike*, in honor of Bob "Spike" Axtel, foreman of the Arizona ranch where Clark spent what probably were the happiest years of his life.

Until "Spanish Is the Lovin' Tongue" appeared on the national scene as a song, Clark's most widely circulated piece was "A Cowboy's Prayer," also written in Arizona and first published in the *Pacific Monthly* for December, 1906. But in spite of its widespread popularity,

Badger Clark snapped in his cabin
at Custer State Park in the Black
Hills of South Dakota. Courtesy of
Badger Clark Memorial Center,
Dakota Wesleyan University.

this one did virtually nothing for the poet, either reputationwise or financially. In a 1956 letter to a friend Clark told how postcard companies all over the West had borrowed his lines and printed them with the notation "Author Unknown." When the actual author or his publisher complained, they usually were informed that the poem had been around for ages and that Badger Clark was just one of a number of old-timers who thought they wrote it. At one time the poet had a collection of more than sixty "A Cowboy's Prayer" postcards that had been sent to him by interested admirers who felt he should be apprised of this poem rustling. Here is the version which appeared in *Sun and Saddle Leather*:

Oh Lord, I've never lived where churches grow.
I love creation better as it stood
That day You finished it so long ago
And looked upon Your work and called it good.
I know that others find You in the light
That's sifted down through tinted window panes,
And yet I seem to feel You near tonight
In this dim, quiet starlight on the plains.

I thank You, Lord, that I am placed so well,
That You have made my freedom so complete;
That I'm no slave of whistle, clock or bell,
Nor weak-eyed prisoner of wall and street.
Just let me live my life as I've begun
And give me work that's open to the sky;
Make me a pardner of the wind and sun,
And I won't ask a life that's soft or high.

Let me be easy on the man that's down;
Let me be square and generous with all.
I'm careless sometimes, Lord, when I'm in town,
But never let 'em say I'm mean or small!
Make me as big and open as the plains,
As honest as the hawse between my knees,
Clean as the wind that blows behind the rains,
Free as the hawk that circles down the breeze!

Forgive me, Lord, if sometimes I forget.
You know about the reasons that are hid.
You understand the things that gall and fret;
You know me better than my mother did.
Just keep an eye on all that's done and said
And right me, sometimes, when I turn aside,
And guide me on the long, dim trail ahead
That stretches upward toward the Great Divide.[6]

NOTES

An earlier version of this chapter appeared in *Arizona Highways*, 45, no. 2 (Feb., 1969), 30–32, 34.

1. This edition is available from the Badger Clark Memorial Center, Dakota Wesleyan University, Mitchell, S.D. 57301, and from Westerners International, University Station, P. O. Box 3941, Tucson, Ariz. 85717.

2. Charles Badger Clark, *Sun and Saddle Leather* (1915; revised, Stockton, Calif.: Westerners Foundation, 1962), pp. 77–80. Glenn Ohrlin gives one tune for "High Chin Bob" in *The Hell-Bound Train: A Cowboy Songbook* (Urbana: University of Illinois Press, 1973), pp. 120–22, and Harlan Daniel cites additional versions in his biblio-discography (p. 266).

3. Romaine Lowdermilk substituted "Yet I keep her memory bright" for this line.

4. Letter from Bill Simon to me, May 9, 1968.

5. Clark, *Sun and Saddle Leather*, p. 39.

6. Ibid., pp. 50–51.

12

The Strange Career
of "The Strawberry Roan"

Of all the songs and poems about bucking horses, the most popular by far among lovers of western balladry is "The Strawberry Roan," an unvarnished tale of a bragging bronc peeler who meets his match in a picturesque and unusual piece of horseflesh. Written by Curley W. Fletcher (1892–1954), a California cowpuncher born in San Francisco and reared in the Owens Valley near Bishop, this has become one of our best-known cowboy songs—one that can be heard on a score of records and found in dozens of books of representative American folk music, more often than not without any credit whatever to the imaginative man who started it all.

Fletcher originally called his fast-moving narrative "The Outlaw Broncho." It appeared under this title in the *Arizona Record* at Globe on December 16, 1915, introduced with the following editorial comment: "Curley Fletcher, well known Western poet and promoter of the Gila Valley Stampede, which is to be given here soon, has kindly consented to allow another of his virile poems to be published for the benefit of Arizona Record's subscribers." The editor added that "The Outlaw Broncho" was in the vernacular and had been printed a number of times by prominent magazines.[1]

Two years later, Fletcher polished up his bucking horse yarn, changed its title to "The Strawberry Roan," and published it in a collection of his original poems called *Rhymes of the Roundup* (1917), which he and his younger brother Fred peddled at rodeos throughout the West.[2] Some unknown balladeer soon worked out a good tune for "Strawberry Roan," and by the mid-twenties it was attracting the attention of folksong collectors. *Century Magazine* printed a variant in

Curley Fletcher (1892–1954).

May of 1925, in an article by Freda Kirchwey, later editor of the *Nation*, who attributed its authorship to a Wyoming dude wrangler identified only as "Charlie." In 1930 Stanford University Press published a book, *I Married a Ranger*, by Dama Margaret Smith (Mrs. "White Mountain" Smith), which printed the song as sung at Grand Canyon by "Ranger Winess."[3]

In 1931 New York theatergoers who attended the Lynn Riggs play *Green Grow the Lilacs*, starring Franchot Tone, heard "The Strawberry Roan" sung by Everett Cheetham, a New Mexico cowboy who had picked it up while working as a guide at Arizona's Castle Hot Springs. The song booklet for the play was issued that year by theatrical publisher Samuel French, with Everett Cheetham's picture on the cover. This booklet for *Green Grow the Lilacs*, forerunner of the phenomenal musical *Oklahoma*, included the tale of the famous bucker, with no clue as to its origin.

Meanwhile, the late Romaine Lowdermilk and a musical group called the Arizona Wranglers had been singing "The Strawberry Roan" repeatedly for appreciative audiences in Phoenix at the Arizona

Biltmore Hotel and over local radio station KTAR. Lowdermilk—rancher, writer, and noted entertainer—believed he was the first to put the song on the air from pioneer Phoenix station KFAD.[4] But he made no claim to having turned Fletcher's poem into a song. He obtained the ballad in the early twenties from a singing Montana cowboy named Mark Tracy, who was killed shortly afterward by a fall from a horse while working for the Hayes Cattle Company at Yarnell, Arizona. Until his death in 1970, Romaine treasured a copy of Fletcher's collected poems, *Songs of the Sage* (1931), whose flyleaf is inscribed in Curley's handwriting: "To my friend Romaine Lowdermilk who is responsible for the popularity of my old Strawberry Roan."[5]

By the early 1930s Curley Fletcher's down-to-earth word-picture of a day in the life of a horsebreaker had indeed become popular. In fact, it had become famous. But very little of its fame had brushed off on its originator. Fletcher was in the unenviable position of having written a poem good enough to be turned into a regional hit tune, only to see it disseminated widely by word of mouth before it was published by an established music house with that all-important copyright notice attached.

Because he was getting neither cash nor credit for his creation, Curley in 1931 settled in Los Angeles and joined forces with Nat Vincent and Fred Howard, a professional Hollywood songwriting and acting team known to radio audiences as the Happy Chappies. Fletcher hoped to regain control of his composition and earn royalties through publishing it, but from his standpoint, it all turned out to be a mistake. The fine old cowboy tale came out of the hopper in 1931 in a sheet music edition copyrighted by Vincent, Howard, and Preeman. It had numerous changes in the wording and a chorus beginning "Oh that Strawberry Roan,/Oh that Strawberry Roan." Luckily for those who preferred their cowboy songs undoctored, Curley was able to talk his collaborators into printing his original poem on the inside back cover, with this explanatory note: "Anyone preferring to sing this version of 'The Strawberry Roan' can do so by using the tune as printed in this copy and omitting the chorus."[6]

The collaboration ended in a legal hassle. But in spite of a contract that entitled the professionals to equal billing with Curley on the sheet music and in a Universal movie called *Strawberry Roan*, in which Ken Maynard sang the song, Fletcher somehow managed to reserve the right to publish the song *his* way in a folio called *Ballads of the Badlands*. This collection of twelve songs was issued in 1932 by the Frontier Publishing Company, without professional assistance and with "The Strawberry Roan" credited only to himself.[7]

This sheet-music edition of "The Strawberry Roan" issued in 1931 was intended to appeal to lovers of "horse operas" featuring singing cowboys. Cover reproduced by permission of ABC Contemporary Music Publishing.

In Hollywood's world of make-believe, the cowboy poet was out of his element and often an unhappy man. One day when he was fed up with the film capital and lawsuits, he wrote me a letter which concluded with these nostalgic lines: "Hell, I was born and reared here in the West. My earliest memory is of cowmen and cattle. I spent my best years as a cowboy of the old school. I knew every water hole, I think, from the Sierra Nevada to Utah. And I still look back to long days and nights in the saddle, at $30 a month, as the happiest of my existence."[8]

Granger's Index to Poetry, a standard reference work found in most public libraries, lists "The Strawberry Roan," says its author is unknown, and refers the reader to *American Ballads and Folk Songs* by John A. and Alan Lomax. However, a reader examining an edition of this fine volume printed within the last twenty or so years will look in vain for the song about the noted bucker.

In 1934 the Lomaxes included "The Strawberry Roan" in the first edition of their *American Ballads and Folk Songs*, with this footnote: "Words dictated by 'Whistle,' a cowboy at Camp Wood, Arizona, August 1929, to Mrs. Janice Reed Lit, Haverford, Pennsylvania."[9] When Curley Fletcher spotted this, he wrote ballad collector John A. Lomax a blistering two-page letter. After outlining the history of the poem and listing the dates of its first appearances in print, Fletcher exploded with the following: "Any one laying claim to having heard or read Strawberry Roan prior to those dates above mentioned is a damned liar, branded so in the eyes of God, myself, himself and the devil."[10]

But things were smoothed over in subsequent correspondence, and in 1938 the Lomaxes brought out a revised and enlarged edition of *Cowboy Songs and Other Frontier Ballads*. The edition contained "The Strawberry Roan" with the footnote about cowboy Whistle and an additional footnote stating that Curley W. Fletcher had composed the original poem and through his courtesy the widely sung narrative was being published again. While this cleared up any misunderstandings insofar as Fletcher was concerned, the song disappeared from later printings of both books. Presumably the M. M. Cole Publishing Company of Chicago, to whom the Vincent-Howard copyright had been assigned in 1935, requested royalties that the Lomaxes or their publisher did not choose to pay.[11]

Curley Fletcher's authorship of his best-known poem once was challenged in print by an itinerant cowboy troubadour and poet named Powder River Jack Lee, who hailed from Deer Lodge, Montana. In 1934 Lee published a song folio which contained "The Strawberry Roan," with a statment that the text was the work of one Frank Chamberlain of Burbank, California. Lee said Chamberlain had written the

The rider about to mount this blindfolded horse is in for the same kind of action provided by the notorious bucker in Curley Fletcher's "Strawberry Roan." The drawing is from a page of western subjects signed C. M. Russell and J. H. Smith which appeared in *Frank Leslie's Illustrated Newspaper* for May 18, 1889. For a few years Smith was well known as an accurate interpreter of the frontier scene, but he became a victim of the wanderlust and never built up a lasting reputation like that eventually achieved by cowboy artist Charles Russell.

poem in 1894 at William Clanton's Laurel Leaf Ranch, at the headwaters of the Moreau River, in South Dakota. He added that a cowboy named Ray Gilbert suggested the theme, and Chamberlain "used it as a recitation for many years while touring the world with his rope-spinning act." Powder River Jack made other extravagant claims in the same book. For example, he stated that he himself was the originator of the famous verses "Tying the Knots in the Devil's Tail," written by Gail I. Gardner of Prescott, Arizona. I knew Jack Lee and am convinced that he suffered from an overactive imagination.[12]

Although no one else has attempted to cast doubt on Curley's claim to "The Strawberry Roan," unfortunately he still gets little or no recognition for his work. In spite of having been included in three printed collections of original Fletcher poems, having been published in sheet music and several copyrighted song folios with his name attached, and having been the subject of a Hollywood lawsuit, in recent years the tale of old roaney has turned up quite regularly in collections of American songs without even a "Thank you, Mr. Fletcher" from the compilers.

Curley had the ideal background for turning out poems smelling authentically of corral dust and saddle leather. According to his brother Fred of San Jose, California, he learned the bronco buster's dangerous trade in his teens while teamed up with a group of Indians catching the wild horses then numerous in the sparsely settled Owens Valley. He soon became a working cowboy, then a busy rodeo contestant and promoter. In a bulldogging contest he lost most of the sight of one eye to a horn, when a steer tossed its head just as he leaped for it. Like many other veterans of the rodeo game, he walked with a limp.

At various times in his life Curley was a mule skinner, prospector, writer of dialogue for Hollywood westerns, musician, magazine editor and columnist, author of two books of humorous prose, and, of course, always a poet. His later years were spent in locating and developing mineral properties in southern California, including operating a tungsten mine at Darwin during World War II. While several of his strikes brought him real money, he had difficulty hanging onto it. With his generous, openhanded nature, he was a soft touch for any old-timer down on his luck. When he passed away at San Jose in 1954 at the age of sixty-two, Curley Fletcher was richer in friends than in worldly goods.

As the following version of the poem "The Strawberry Roan" is somewhat of a historical document, it is reproduced here (with obvious typographical errors corrected) exactly as printed more than half a century ago, with all its peculiarities and inconsistencies in spelling included. Titled "The Outlaw Broncho," it appeared in the *Arizona Record* (Globe) on December 16, 1915, and was signed by Curley W. Fletcher. The melody is that recorded by Nubbins of the Arizona Wranglers some forty-five years ago.[13]

Git Along, Little Dogies

_____ uh bronc fight-er by the looks o' yer clothes." Well I
thought he was right _ and I told him the same, Then I
asks has he got _ an-y bad ones to tame. _ He _
says he has one a bad one tuh buck, And fur
pil - ing good cow - boys he has lots_ uh luck.

I was loafin' around just spendin' muh time
Out of a job and I hadn't a dime,
When a feller steps up and sez he "I suppose
That yore uh bronc fighter by the looks o' yer clothes."

Well I thought he was right and I told him the same,
Then I asks has he got any bad ones to tame.
He says he has one a bad one tuh buck,
And fur piling good cowboys he has lots uh luck.

Well I gets all excited and asks what he pays,
Tuh ride that old pony a couple uh days.
He offers ten dollars. Sez I "I'm yure man,
Fur the bronk never lived that I couldn't fan."[14]

I don't like to brag but I got this tuh say,
That I ain't been throwed fur many a day.
Sez he git yur saddle I'll give yuh a chance,
So I gits in his buckboard and drifts tuh his ranch.

I stays until mornin' and right after chuck,
I steps out tuh see if that outlaw kin buck.
He was down in the hoss corral standing alone,
A snakey eyed outlaw, a strawberry roan.

"The Strawberry Roan"

His legs is all spavined he's got pigeon toes,
Little pig eyes and a long roman nose,
Little pin ears that touched at the tip,
An X.Y.Z. iron stamped on his hip.

Yew necked[15] he is with a long lower jaw,
All the things that you'll see on a wild outlaw.
Well I puts on muh spurs I'm sure feelin' fine,
Turns up muh hat and picks up muh twine.[16]

I dabs that loop on him and well I knows then,
That before he is rode I'll sure earn that ten.
I gets muh blinds[17] on him it shore is a fight,
Next comes muh saddle I screws it down tight.

Then I gets on him I sez "Raise the blind,
Move out uv his way and les see him unwind."
Well he bows his old neck and I guess he unwound,
Fur he ain't spendin' much uv his time on the ground.

He turns his old belly right up to the sun,
He shore is a sunfishing[18] sun-of-a-gun.
He goes up toward the east and comes down toward the west,
To stay on his middle I'm doin' muh best.

He is the worst bucker I sees on the range,
He could turn on a dime and give you back change.
He hits on all fours and turns up on his side,
I don't see how he keeps from sheddin' his hide.

I tell yuh, no foolin', that caballo[19] can step,
I was still in my saddle, abuildin' some rep.
Away goes muh stirrups and I loses muh hat,
I'm grabbin' the apple[20] and blind as a bat.

He shore is frog walkin'[21] he heaves a big sigh,
He only lacks wings fur tuh be on the fly.
An while he's a bucking he squeals like a shoat,
I tell yuh that pony has shore got muh goat.

With a phenominal jump he kicks her in high,[22]
And I'm settin' on nothin' way up in the sky.
And then I descends, I comes back tuh earth,
And I lights inta cussin' the day of his birth.

Then I knows that the hosses I ain't able tuh ride,
Is some uv them livin', they haven't all died.
And I bets all muh money that no man alive,
Can stay with that bronk when he makes that high dive.

Evidently there is something magical about Curley Fletcher's "Strawberry Roan." Parodies and imitations of it abound in the West, with labels such as "The Fate of the Strawberry Roan," "He Rode the Strawberry Roan," "Good-bye Old Strawberry Roan," and the ultimate, "The Strawberry Blonde on the Strawberry Roan." In Ohio there is even a Pennsylvania Dutch version called "Die Apbarre Roan." Curley himself wrote two songs with the same meter and rhyme scheme as the poem that became so famous. These are "The Ridge Running Roan," published in his 1931 volume of poems, *Songs of the Sage*, and "The Bad Brahma Bull," written in 1933 and originally called "The Flyin' U Twister."[23]

NOTES

An earlier version of this chapter appeared in *Arizona and the West*, 11 (Winter, 1969), 359–66.

1. The editor probably exaggerated. On April 29, 1934, Curley wrote me that "The Outlaw Broncho" had been published in the *Boulder Creek* (Calif.) *News* in March of 1914 but made no mention of its having been printed elsewhere.

2. *Rhymes of the Roundup* was printed by the Shannon-Conmy Printing Company (San Francisco). In a letter to me dated May 12, 1934, Fletcher stated that 5,000 copies were issued.

3. Freda Kirchwey, "The Birth of a Ballad: A Note on a Cow-Boy Minstrel," *Century Magazine*, 110 (May, 1925), 23–24; Dama Margaret Smith, *I Married a Ranger* (Stanford, Calif.: Stanford University Press, 1930), pp. 82–84.

4. The tune used for "The Strawberry Roan" by Nubbins (J. E. Patterson) of the Arizona Wranglers appears at the end of this chapter. For more on Lowdermilk see chapter 9.

5. *Songs of the Sage*, a small hard-cover edition of Curley's original poems, including "The Strawberry Roan," was issued by the Frontier Publishing Company of Los Angeles. Lowdermilk's information on Tracy was confirmed by Roy Hayes, head of the Hayes Cattle Company at Yarnell, in a letter to me dated August 30, 1968.

6. The ASCAP *Biographical Dictionary of Composers, Authors and Publishers* (New York: American Society of Authors, Composers and Publishers, 1966), pp. 347 and 755, credits Vincent and Howard with the authorship of "The Strawberry Roan." In 1935 the copyright was assigned to the M. M. Cole Publishing Company of Chicago.

7. Included was "The Ridge Running Roan," used in the Universal picture *Stormy* and later published with five other Curley Fletcher songs in a Tex Ritter song folio issued in 1941 by M. M. Cole (Chicago).

8. Letter from Curley Fletcher to me, May 12, 1934.

9. John A. Lomax and Alan Lomax, *American Ballads and Folk Songs* (New York: Macmillan Co., 1934), p. 392.

10. Curley Fletcher fired off his letter of complaint to John A. Lomax on December 28, 1934, and sent a copy to me.

11. John A. Lomax and Alan Lomax, *Cowboy Songs and Other Frontier Ballads*, rev. and enl. (New York: Macmillan Co., 1938), pp. 99–102. Fletcher gave his permission in a letter to John A. Lomax dated October 26, 1937. Writing on the letterhead of *Ride*, a magazine published in Hollywood, Curley added that he was currently the editor of the publication and "principal contributor under numerous nom de plumes."

12. *Powder River Jack and Kitty Lee's Cowboy Song Book* (Butte, Mont.: McKee Printing Co., 1934). Jack Lee was killed in an Arizona auto mishap in 1945. Lee's book also contained two poems from E. A. Brininstool's *Trail Dust of a Maverick* (New York: Dodd Mead, 1914). These were "The Old Yellow Slicker" and "Corral Soliloquy," worked over slightly—the first credited to Lee, the second to a Kearney Moore. Badger Clark's poem "From Town" was credited to one Seven Anderton. As for "Tying a Knot in the Devil's Tail" (Lee's title), Lee published this several times as his own work after recording it for Victor in 1930 (Victor 23527, reissued on *Authentic*

Cowboys and Their Western Folksongs, RCA Victor LPV 522); Powder River Jack wrote me on March 27, 1934, that he had composed the poem in 1892. For its true history see chapter 10.

13. *Those Fabulous "Beverly Hill Billies"* (Rare Arts Records WLP 1000).

14. *Fan*—A bronc rider would often take his hat and "fan" the horse from side to side to show his complete mastery of the situation. Or he might sit there and "fan" himself to show his nonchalance.

15. *Yew necked*—Fletcher probably meant *ewe-necked*, although in subsequent printings of the poem he never changed the spelling. A great many variants use *ewe-necked*.

16. *Twine*—rope, lariat.

17. *Blinds*—a blindfold, usually made of leather, which covered the animal's eyes while the saddle was being put on.

18. *Sunfishin'*—In *The Old-Time Cowhand* (New York: Macmillan Co., 1961), p. 298, Ramon F. Adams states that a sunfisher "was a hoss that twisted his body into a crescent, or, in other words, when he seemed to try to touch the gound with first one shoulder and then the other, lettin' the sunlight hit his belly. Such pitchin' was called 'sunfishin'.'"

19. *Caballo*—Spanish for "horse."

20. *Grabbin' the apple*—grabbing the saddle horn. In *The Book of the American West*, ed. Jay Monaghan (New York: Julian Messner, 1963), pp. 335–36, Ramon F. Adams explains that the apple-horn saddle came into use in the early 1880s. The horn, made of metal, usually with a leather cover, was about the size of a small apple.

21. *Frog walkin'*—In *The Old-Time Cowhand*, Adams says a horse that jumped about with arched back and stiffened knees was said to "frog walk" or "crow hop" (p. 300).

22. *Kicks her in high*—This may be an analogy with operating the famed Model T Ford, which had three pedals—forward, reverse, and brake. You pressed the forward pedal for low gear, then just kicked your foot off it; the pedal slipped back into high and you were on your way.

23. "Strawberry Roan" buffs can be grateful to Austin E. Fife for assembling these and other texts in "The Strawberry Roan and His Progeny," *John Edwards Memorial Foundation Quarterly*, 8 (Autumn, 1972), 149–65. This article carries a bibliography and a discography for old Strawberry and his offspring. See also Harlan Daniel's notes in Glenn Ohrlin, *The Hell-Bound Train: A Cowboy Songbook* (Urbana: University of Illinois Press, 1973), pp. 260–61.

13

"The Zebra Dun"

As the bucking horse has been a fact of life with the American cowboy from the very start of the cattle industry through today's commercialized rodeo, it is only natural that there should be songs on the subject. One side of the coin is presented in "The Strawberry Roan," Curley Fletcher's fast-moving drama of a cocky horsebreaker who, for all his bragging, has the humbling experience of landing in the dirt.[1] "The Zebra Dun" gives the other side. Usually sung to an old Irish air, "The Son of a Gambolier," it tells of a supposed tenderfoot who neatly turns the tables and gives a lesson in equitation to the practical jokers who have assigned him their outfit's worst four-footed outlaw.[2]

The origin of this popular western ballad is a mystery. Its first known appearance in print was in *Songs of the Cowboys*, a slim booklet with the words of twenty-three songs issued in 1908 at Estancia, New Mexico, by N. Howard "Jack" Thorp. He printed only nine stanzas and gave them the title "Educated Feller." In 1910 a 12½-stanza version was included in the first John Lomax collection, *Cowboy Songs and Other Frontier Ballads*. Lomax's title was "The Zebra Dun."[3]

The variant of "The Zebra Dun" given below was quoted by Dane Coolidge, author of numerous books on the West, in his 1912 article "Cow Boy Songs." Coolidge said he had obtained the song from Sam Roberts, a C-Bar cowpuncher at Dragoon Station in Cochise County, Arizona. In the article Coolidge described a zebra dun as "a buckskin horse with zebra stripes on his legs, an old Spanish breed reputed to be great broncos." The tune is the one I sang on "Death Valley Days" for more than five years.[4]

"The Zebra Dun"

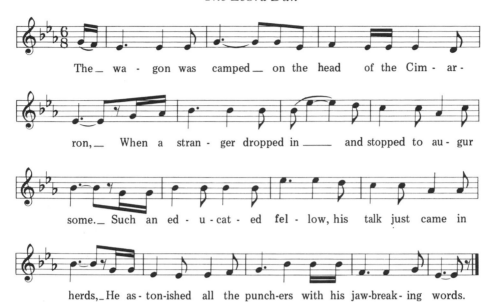

The _ wa - gon was camped _ on the head of the Cim - ar -
ron, _ When a stran - ger dropped in ____ and stopped to au - gur
some. _ Such an ed - u - cat - ed fel - low, his talk just came in
herds, _ He as - ton - ished all the punch-ers with his jaw-break - ing words.

The wagon was camped on the head of the Cimarron,
When a stranger dropped in and stopped to augur[5] some.
Such an educated fellow, his talk just came in herds,
He astonished all the punchers with his jawbreaking words.

We asked him if he'd had his breakfast and he hadn't had a sniff,
So we opened up the chuck-box and bid him help himself.
He helped himself to beefsteak, a biscuit and some beans,
And then began to talk about the foreign kings and queens.

He talked about the Spanish war and fighting on the seas,
With guns as big as beef-steers and ramrods big as trees.
He spoke about old Dewey, that fighting son-of-a-gun,
And said he was the bravest cuss that ever pulled a gun.

He kept on talking till he made the boys all sick;
And they tried to figure up some way to play a trick.
He said he'd lost his job up close to Santa Fe,
And was cutting across the country to strike the 7 Ds.

Didn't say what was the matter, but some trouble with the boss,
And wanted to know if he could borrow a fresh, fat saddle horse.
That tickled all the boys, they laughed down in their sleeves,
We told him he could have one as fresh and fat as he pleased.

Shorty grabbed the lasso and roped old Zebra Dun,
Turned him over to the stranger and stepped back to see the fun.
Old Dun he was a rocky outlaw that had grown so awful wild,
He could paw the white out of the moon for a quarter of a mile.

Old Dunny stood quite gentle as if he didn't know
That the stranger had him saddled and was fixing for to go.
When the stranger hit the saddle, old Dunny quit the earth,
Traveled up towards the moon for everything he was worth.

We could see the tops of all the trees under old Dunny's belly every
    jump,
But the stranger he was growed there just like a camel's hump.
He spurred him in the shoulders and whipped him as he whirled,
Just to show us flunky punchers he was the wolf of the world.

He sat up on old Dunny and curled his long mustache,
Just like a summer boarder a-waiting for his hash.
When his hind feet were perpendicular and fore ones on the bits,
He spurred him in the shoulders till old Dunny had wall-eyed fits.

When old Dunny was all through pitching and the stranger was on
    the ground
The rest of us punchers were gathered close around.
The boss said, "If you can throw the lasso like you can ride old Dun
You are the man I've been looking for ever since the year of one."

Well, I can throw the lasso, neither do I do it slow,
I can catch their fore pins nine times out of ten for any kind of
    dough.
But there's one thing sure and certain I've learned since I've been
    born,
The educated fellows ain't all greenhorns.

When writing on cowboy songs in the *Saturday Evening Post* for
June 27, 1925, Will Croft Barnes, veteran rancher, author, and conservationist, described a zebra dun as "an animal generally of a claybank
or buckskin shade, with dark zebra stripes across his withers and
around both forelegs." Author Barnes further commented: "Many
cowboys believed sincerely that the mother of a zebra dun had mule
blood in her system. They were perhaps entitled to this belief because,
as one cowboy put it, 'a zebra dun hoss is the toughest, wickedest, most
devlish-tempered brute that ever felt a cinch on his belly or crippled up
a pore cow person.' "[6]

Apparently unaware of this expert testimony from two extremely
well-qualified observers of the western scene, folklorist Margaret Larkin, in her fine song collection *Singing Cowboy*, published in 1931,
announced that the famous ballad actually did not involve a zebra dun
horse. Although admitting that the song's origin was unknown to her,
she printed this puzzling statement: "The bronco of the song was a
dun-colored horse bearing the Z Bar brand. His name was easily
corrupted and nowadays the singing cowboys call him Zebra Dun."[7]

An outlaw horse drawn by twenty-five-year-old Charles M. Russell for *Frank Leslie's Illustrated Newspaper*, May 18, 1889.

Miss Larkin's book was the first hard-cover collection of exclusively western music to have piano arrangements for every song included. And for each of the forty entries she supplied interesting comments concerning the song's origin or background. Her volume greatly influenced later songbook editors, several of whom unfortunately enlarged on her remarks about zebra duns. They went so far as to spread the word that there never was any such animal.

In the interest of setting the record straight, when I was preparing an article on "The Zebra Dun" that appeared in the Sunday magazine section of the *Arizona Republic* (Phoenix) for March 9, 1969, I wrote to three of my friends in the Southwest (all of whom happen to be subjects of chapters in this book), and asked whether they ever had seen a zebra dun horse. Their replies left little doubt that there *is* such a critter. This is what they said:

"One of the best horses I ever owned was a zebra dun, marked as Will Barnes says and with a black stripe down his back also."—Gail I. Gardner (Prescott, Arizona).[8]

"I have seen a couple of zebra duns in my life. They were a dark dun, yellowish-brown base color with black mane and tail and black stripes on the lower legs and faintly striped across the withers. They are 'tough as a boot and rough as a woodpile.' You never could tell when they would start bucking. Usually they are long-lived. I knew of one with a lot of mustang blood in him that lived to be forty-two years old."—Carl T. Sprague (Bryan, Texas).[9]

"I had a zebra dun horse—close-coupled, tireless, eager with roping or cutting, sure-footed, with little bat ears always working. He had zebra stripes down his withers and around both forelegs. Also a jack-stripe down his rump and onto his tail. He was from wild stock but broke gentle to ride and drive to a light buggy. I don't think the color of a horse has anything to do with his temperament. But any zebra dun is a good horse to have—lots of bottom. But they can be spoiled just like any other color if you're careless when breaking."—Romaine H. Lowdermilk (Phoenix, Arizona).[10]

When Prescott's Bill Simon heard about the preparation of this book, he volunteered a bit more information that seems to make the zebra dun story complete and possibly qualifies every reader of these pages as an expert on oddly marked cowhorses. Says Bill: "There are not only zebra dun horses but zebra browns and zebra bays also. I rode an old snake up at the Double O Ranch years ago. They called him Scar Leg. He had no scars on him, but there were black rings on his forelegs and a black stripe the full length of his back. I would have liked to scar him up with my spurs but it was all I could do to ride hangin' fire."[11] My dictionary defines *hanging fire* as "unsettled or undecided," which about describes Bill's situation.

NOTES

An earlier version of this chapter appeared in the *Arizona Republic* (Phoenix) Sunday supplement, March 9, 1969.

1. See chapter 12.

2. In his introduction to "Zebra Dun" in *The Hell-Bound Train: A Cowboy Songbook* (Urbana: University of Illinois Press, 1973), pp. 54–57, Glenn Ohrlin tells about famous bronc riders who actually pulled this stunt of dressing like a dude. For other appearances of the song see Harlan Daniel's biblio-discography in the same book (pp. 257–58).

3. In 1921 Thorp compiled an enlarged collection, also called *Songs of the Cowboys* (Boston: Houghton Mifflin Co.), which included twelve stanzas titled "The Zebra Dun." An explanatory note said Thorp had first heard it sung in 1890 by Randolph Reynolds at Carrizozo Flats. The Thorp texts, and others, are discussed by Austin and Alta Fife in *Songs of the Cowboys, by N. Howard ("Jack") Thorp* (New York: Clarkson N. Potter, Bramhall House, 1966), pp. 135–47. For more on Thorp and Lomax see chapter 19.

4. Dane Coolidge, "Cow Boy Songs," *Sunset, the Pacific Monthly*, 29 (Nov., 1912), 509–10; John I. White, *Cowboy Songs as Sung by John White "The Lonesome Cowboy" in Death Valley Days* (New York: Pacific Coast Borax Co., 1934).

5. *Augur*—talk.

6. Will Croft Barnes, "The Cowboy and His Songs," *Saturday Evening Post*, June 27, 1925, p.125. For more on Barnes see chapter 6.

7. Margaret Larkin, *Singing Cowboy* (1931; reprinted, New York: Oak Publications, 1963), p. 49.

8. Letter from Gardner to me, Apr. 10, 1967.

9. Letter from Sprague to me, Mar. 21, 1968.

10. Letter from Lowdermilk to me, Apr. 30, 1967.

11. Letter from Bill Simon to me, Aug. 29, 1972. For Bill's contributions to western balladry see chapters 10 and 11.

14

Where the Deer
and the Antelope Play

Thanks largely to the sudden growth of radio broadcasting, in the early 1930s America discovered and took to its heart what it thought was a genuine western folksong. As the haunting, comforting strains "Where seldom is heard a discouraging word / And the skies are not cloudy all day" miraculously came out of the air, the country somehow felt that it had a good thing going, stock market crashes and depressions notwithstanding.

Certainly the music publishers, movie makers, and broadcasting companies had a good thing going. Sheet music versions of the hit tune "Home on the Range," some by well-known composers, others by unknowns, were cascading off the presses. Opera stars, crooners, and garden-variety guitar plunkers like myself were sending it over the airways or putting it on records. Kay Francis was singing it to Edward G. Robinson in a movie called *I Loved a Woman*.[1] Even Rear Admiral Richard E. Byrd was singing it, to himself, during the isolated vigil in Antarctica that almost cost him his life.[2]

In addition to the public's listening at home or in concert halls, loving the song and not getting tired of it, a nice thing about it all was that nobody had to pay royalties to a poet. As an old western folksong, "Home on the Range" was—or so most everyone thought—in the public domain.

Even noted ballad hunter John Avery Lomax, although not cut in on the profits from Tin Pan Alley, must have felt a certain sense of pleasure over the popularity of "Home on the Range." For it was he who had obtained it in 1908 from Bill Jack Curry, a Negro saloonkeeper in San Antonio, formerly a cook with cow outfits.[3] Lomax had pub-

The universal appeal of "Home on the Range" was pointed up in this 1934 cartoon by J. R. Williams. Reprinted by permission of Newspaper Enterprise Association.

lished it, with piano accompaniment, in his anthology *Cowboy Songs and Other Frontier Ballads* in 1910.

Aside from royalties on his book, Lomax missed out on the cash and largely on the credit, too, insofar as the song-buying public was concerned. On examining a dozen sheet music editions of the song that I squirreled away in a closet four decades ago, I find that only one, the very first, arranged by Oscar J. Fox of the Lone Star State and issued in 1925 by Carl Fischer, acknowledged a debt to Lomax, although most of the others bear a close resemblance to his original.

The earliest "Home on the Range" recording of which I have any knowledge is that made by Vernon Dalhart and released by Brunswick in 1927. In 1928 Jules Verne Allen recorded it for Victor.[4]

As I said, with "Home on the Range" the music publishers and others appeared to have a good thing going. But all of a sudden, in the summer of 1934, word went out to ban the song from the air. Someone was claiming that it was not in the public domain after all.

This sour note was being sounded by William Goodwin, a grain dealer in Tempe, Arizona, and his wife, Mary. On June 14, 1934, the Southern Music Publishing Company filed suit with the Federal Court at New York City in the name of the Goodwins, claiming that the currently popular western folksong "Home on the Range" was simply a working-over of the Goodwins' own composition, one called "An Arizona Home," copyrighted in 1905. The complaint named twenty-nine defendants, including a long list of music publishers, two movie companies, the National Broadcasting Company, the Columbia Broadcasting Company, and six individuals, among them this writer, whose only notice that he was in hot water came to him through the newspapers. The Goodwins, asking half a million in damages, were after bigger fish.[5]

Although it never was explained to me, my involvement in this legal action apparently stemmed from one, or both, of two things. In 1929, in cooperation with George Shackley, musical director at radio station WOR, I had brought out a folio, *The Lonesome Cowboy: Songs of the Plains and Hills*, which included "Home on the Range." This was copyrighted by the publisher, Al Piantadosi. Although the reasons escape me completely some forty years later, printed copies in my possession state that in 1930 the copyright was assigned to a firm by the name of Geo. T. Worth & Company. In 1932, without even mentioning it to me, Geo. T. Worth & Company issued "Home on the Range" in sheet music, crediting me with the very nice musical arrangment. Moreover, my name appeared on the front cover three times, which I am sure flattered me no end. But two years later, with the Goodwins including me on their list of alleged copyright infringers, I had some second thoughts.

My notes of forty years ago indicate that David W. Guion, Texas-born radio impresario and an established composer with a reputation for excellent musical arrangements with western settings, was the one individual defendant actually called on by the process server. Living in New York at the time, he probably was easy to find, and it could easily have been proved that he was making money on the song in addition to having done a great deal to popularize it. He was receiving composer's royalties from G. Schirmer for choral and orchestral arrangements of "Home on the Range" as well as for the unique 1930 solo arrangement that was a favorite with concert artists. Unlike most versions, which are quite simple and repetitious, Guion's had a particularly appealing melody for the stanza beginning "Oh, give me a land where the bright diamond sand / Flows leisurely down the stream," which placed his composition in a class by itself.[6]

The Goodwins, to prove their point, submitted to the court "An Arizona Home" in sheet music, copyrighted on February 27, 1905, by the Balmer & Weber Music House of Saint Louis. Goodwin was credited with the words appearing below, his wife with the melody.

Oh give me a home where the buffalos roam, Where the deer and the an-te-lopes play,— Where sel-dom is heard a dis-cour-ag-ing word And the sky is not cloud-y all day.—

CHORUS

A home,— a home,— Where the deer and the an-te-lopes play,—— Where sel-dom is heard a dis-cour-ag-ing word And the sky is not cloud-y all day.—

Oh give me a home where the buffalos roam,
Where the deer and the antelopes play,
Where seldom is heard a discouraging word
And the sky is not cloudy all day.
Yes, give me the gleam of the swift mountain stream
And the place where no hurricanes blow,
Oh give me the park where the prairie dogs bark
And the mountains all covered with snow.

> A home, a home,
> Where the deer and the antelopes play,
> Where seldom is heard a discouraging word
> And the sky is not cloudy all day.

> Oh give me the hills and the ring of the drills
> And the rich silver ore in the ground.
> Yes, give me the gulch where the miners can sluice
> And the bright yellow gold can be found.
> Oh give me the mine where the prospectors find
> The gold in its own native land,
> And the hot springs below, where the sick people go
> And camp on the banks of the Grand.

> Oh give me the steed and the gun that I need
> To shoot game from my own cabin home.
> Then give me the camp where the fire is a lamp
> And the wild rocky mountains to roam.
> Yes, give me the home where the prospectors roam,
> There business is always alive
> In those wild western hills midst the ring of the drills,
> Oh there let me live till I die.

Although half a million probably represented considerably more than the Goodwins actually hoped to get, since their melody and eight lines of their lyrics were almost the same as the universally popular version of "Home on the Range," the matter could not be laughed off. To block their suit, someone had to produce strong evidence, not just the opinions of a few old-timers, that the song was current in the West prior to 1905. Therefore, the music publishers raised a defense fund and hired a New York lawyer, Samuel Moanfeldt, to hunt for the real composer or composers of the song.

Newspaper accounts of the Goodwins' court action had brought in to the Music Publishers Protective Association a helpful letter from a Mrs. Giddeon of Chicago. She stated that in 1880, while attending Normal School at Stanberry, Missouri, she and her classmates had regularly sung "Home on the Range" at school functions. She supplied an affidavit to this effect and also gave attorney Moanfeldt the names of fellow students still living in Missouri who did likewise. But none recalled ever having seen the song in print or had thought of writing the words in a diary.[7]

Because "Home on the Range" was generally considered a cowboy song, Moanfeldt next tried Dodge City, Kansas, once the world's leading cattle market. His findings there are described in his report to his client.

There I interviewed a great number of people such as ex-cowboys, people who were employed as cooks in cowboy camps, ex–stage drivers and buffalo hunters. A great number of written statements were procured by me from these people and they all agreed that this song was well known to and generally sung by cowboys and other people traveling through that section of the country in stage coaches prior to 1890, and that the lyrics and music were practically identical with those now generally used by radio singers, and they all stated that they recognized the tune as soon as the same became popular over the radio.[8]

The lawyer–turned–tune detective had a pocketful of potentially valuable affidavits but still nothing on the song's origin. Now, following up another clue, he explored a different field—central Colorado.

By the strangest of coincidences, a short time prior to the filing of the Goodwins' complaint, another claimant for the honor of having had a hand in the composition of "Home on the Range" had come forward. He was Bob Swartz of Scranton, Pennsylvania, who in 1885 had tried his luck at mining near Leadville in the mountains southwest of Denver. On August 14, 1930, Swartz addressed a letter to me saying that hearing me sing "Home on the Range" from a station in New York had stirred old memories. To my surprise and, I suspect, to my disbelief, he stated that forty-five years earlier he and two fellow miners had composed the song I had been singing.

Swartz died on March 12, 1932, before he could make much of a case. However, a sister in Pennsylvania had saved a dated letter written by him in 1885 in which he had proudly put down the lyrics to a song he called "Colorado Home," and he himself had produced an old notebook with a melody he claimed to have written down in the late 1880s shortly after he gave up mining and returned to the East. Music historian and composer Kenneth S. Clark interested himself in the matter and with the cooperation of the Paull-Pioneer Music Corporation of New York published the complete story in an insert to a sheet music edition of "Colorado Home" in 1934. The Swartz melody was essentially the one so familiar today. With the exception of two lines, the text was almost identical with that claimed to have been written by Goodwin. In place of Goodwin's last two lines, Swartz contributed this far more virile description:

> Where dance halls come first and faro banks burst,
> And every saloon is a dive.

In Colorado, too, attorney Moanfeldt experienced little difficulty locating numerous senior citizens who recalled having heard the song half a century earlier. He concluded that Swartz and his buddies had

COLORADO HOME
PROSPECTORS' SONG
The Original of "HOME ON THE RANGE"
Together with the Entire Story of the Writing of the Song in 1885
and Including Reproductions of the Original Manuscript

MUSIC BY
C.O.(Bob) SWARTZ
WORDS BY
BILL McCABE, BINGHAM GRAVES, C.O. SWARTZ,
"Jim" and Others

BOB SWARTZ

As He Appeared as a Prospector in Colorado at the Time of the Writing of "Colorado Home" in 1885 - From a Portrait Sent East to His Family During That Period.

LOCALE WHERE THE SONG WAS WRITTEN

The Cabin Marked No. 1 Was "Junk Lane Hotel", near Leadville, Colorado, in Which "Colorado Home" Was Composed by the Storm-Bound Prospectors During the Winter of 1885. All the Points of Interest, as Marked by Numbers, Were Identified on the Back of This Picture Received by the Swartz Family at the Time.

PUBLISHED BY **PAULL-PIONEER MUSIC C**ᵒʳᵖ **119-FIFTH AVE.**
NEW YORK

Front cover reproduced by courtesy of the publisher. © Copyright 1934, Shawnee Press, Inc., Delaware Water Gap, Pennsylvania 18327. U.S. Copyright renewed 1962.

Left, Ohio-born Dr. Brewster Higley (1823–1911), Kansas pioneer; *below*, Daniel E. Kelley (1843–1905), Rhode Island Civil War veteran, musician, and entertainer, credited with having turned Dr. Higley's poem "Western Home" into the song that in the early 1930s became world famous as "Home on the Range" and in 1947 was made the official state song of Kansas. Courtesy of the Kansas State Historical Society, Topeka.

taken the tune and a snatch of the words of an older song and made up verses to fit their own situation high in the Rockies—a common enough occurrence in those days among people living in isolated regions of the country. Where the Goodwins picked up the song is still a mystery. As Moanfeldt pointed out in his report, their lyrics seem much more at home in Colorado than in Arizona.[9]

Moanfeldt now probably had all he needed to nullify the Goodwin action. But he was not satisfied. Finding the original of "Home on the Range" was still a challenge.

In March of 1935 a Dodge City newspaper had obligingly run an item about the controversy with an appeal for information on the song's origin. Picked up and circulated widely by the Associated Press, this brought a response from Mrs. Myrtle Hose of Osborne, Kansas, who had a scrapbook containing a 1914 newspaper clipping with the words of "Home on the Range" and a statement that they were being reprinted from an issue of the same paper run off in 1873. They had been written, the editor stated, by his friend Dr. Brewster Higley. The paper was the *Smith County Pioneer*, published at Smith Center on the northern Kansas prairies.

Unfortunately, no copy of the all-important 1873 issue of the *Pioneer* could be found in its files or ever was found elsewhere. However, from the available evidence and from conversations with early Smith County settlers, Moanfeldt was convinced that the poem, originally called "Western Home," had indeed been written by Ohio-born Higley, an eccentric physician who had homesteaded in Smith County in 1871. Credit for setting it to music went to one of Higley's neighbors, Dan Kelley, a Rhode Island Civil War veteran who went to Kansas in 1872 and made his living as a carpenter and builder.

Among those interviewed in Smith County, Kansas, by attorney Moanfeldt was Clarence R. Harlan, eighty-six years old and blind, brother-in-law of Dan Kelley. Harlan played guitar and with his younger brother, a fiddler, made up the so-called Harlan Orchestra that in early days performed throughout the region for dances and celebrations. Moanfeldt buttressed his evidence with a phonograph record of "Western Home" made by blind Clarence Harlan, who sang the words from memory exactly as they were printed in the 1914 *Pioneer* clipping and stated he had learned the song in 1874. Harlan said that neither he nor his brother had ever written out the melody. Attorney Moanfeldt once played this record for me and allowed me to transcribe the tune. It was in waltz time and close enough to the well-known melody of today as to be recognizable:[10]

Job Printing

THE KIRWIN CHIEF

Job Office,

East side Public Square,

First door south of the Post-office, Kirwin, Kan.

Kirwin Chief.

W. D. & C. T. JENKINS, Proprietors.

"Fearless and Free."

$1.50 per year, in Advance

VOL. 3.   KIRWIN KANSAS, SATURDAY FEBRUARY 26. 1876.   NO. 14.

RATES OF ADVERTISING.

1 column one year	$105.00
½ " "	$55.00
¼ " "	$30.00
1 " 6 months	$55.00
Professional Cards, per year	$5.00
Local Notices	$4.00

All legal notices must be paid for in advance or they will not be inserted.

Rates of Subscription.

One copy 1 year	$1.50
One copy 6 months	1.00
One copy 3 months	.50

15 cents extra will be charged for papers going out of the county.

PLAGIARISM.

The editor of the Stockton *News* has allowed himself to become the victim of an ambitious aspirant for poetical fame. In the issue of Feb. 3d., 1876, he published under the head of "My home in the West" a poem, purporting to have been written by Mrs. Knox-Pierce, of Raceburgh, Rooks county, Kansas. The poem in question—with the exception of two words, was written by Dr. J. R. Higley, of Beaver creek, and first published in the Kirwin Chief, March 31st, 1874. We re-publish the article as written by Dr. Higley, and ask our readers to compare it with the stolen article from Raceburgh. Dr. Higley must look to his laurels, as he will find plenty of people who are willing to profit by the brain work of others.

Western Home.

BY DR. HIGLEY.

Oh! give me a home where the Buffalo roam,
Where the Deer and the Antelope play;
Where never is heard a discouraging word,
An' the sky is not clouded all day.

To those who love the Antelope play,
Where the Deer and the Antelope play,
Where seldom is heard a discouraging word,
And the sky is not clouded all day.

Oh! give me land where the bright diamond sand,
Throws its light from the glittering stream,
Where glideth along the graceful white swan,
Like the maid in her heavenly dreams.

[Chorus] A home! A home!

Oh! give me a gale of the Solomon vale,
Where life the streams with buoyancy flow;
On the banks of the Beaver, where seldom if ever,
Any poisonous herbage doth grow.

[Chorus] A home! A home!

How often at night, when the heavens are bright,
With the light of the twinkling stars,
Have I stood there amazed, and asked as I gazed,
If their glory exceeds that of ours.

[Chorus] A home! A home!

I love the wild flowers in this bright land of ours,
I love the wild curlew's shrill scream,
The bluffs and white rocks, and antelope flocks,
That graze on the mountains so green.

[Chorus] A home! A home!

The air is so pure and the breeze so free,
The zephyrs so balmy and light,
That I would not exchange my home here to range,
Forever in azure so bright.

[Chorus] A home! A home!

"WESTWARD THE MARCH OF EMPIRE TAKES ITS WAY."

I hear the tread of pioneers
Of nations yet to be,
The first low wash of waves, where soon
Shall roll a human sea.

Behind the scared squaw's birch canoe,
The steamer smokes and raves;
And city lots are staked for sale
Above old Indian graves.

No portion of the West offers greater inducements to the farmer, merchant or mechanic, than is to be found in the Kirwin Land District. Good homesteads can yet be secured near all the towns, and the rapid increase in value, will insure a four-fold return of the expense of improvements. To those who intend seeking homes in the west, who want a healthy climate, good soil, good water, good schools and good society, we

The rudiments of Empire here,
The New World in its crude,
Its tipped with fire the day spears
Or mony a mountain chain.

Each rude and jostling fragment soon
Its fitting place shall find,
The raw material of a State,
Its muscle and its mind!

And westward still the star which leads
The New World in its train,
Has tipped with fire the day spears
Or mony a mountain chain.

And lo! thy glorious realm outspread
You stretching valleys green and gray
And yon free hill tops o'er whose brow
The four white clouds are borne away.

HOMESTEAD SCENE IN THE KIRWIN LAND DISTRICT.

The Kansas Emigrant's Song.

Air—Auld Lang Syne.

We cross the prairies as of old
The pilgrims crossed the sea,
To make the West as they the East,
The homestead of the free.

Cho.—The homestead of the free my boys,
The homestead of the free;
To make the West, as they the East,
The homestead of the free.

We go to rear a wall of men
On Freedom's Southern line,
And plant beside the cotton tree,
The rugged Northern pine!

We're flowing from our native hills,
As our free rivers flow;
The blessing of our mother-land
Is on us as we go.

We go to plant our common schools
On distant prairie swells,
And give the Sabbaths of the wild,
The music of its bells.

Upbearing like the ark of old,
The bible in our van,
We go to test the truth of God
Against the fraud of men.

No pause, nor rest, save where the
streams that feed the Kansas run,
Save where our pilgrim gonfalon
Shall flout the setting sun.

We'll sweep the prairies as of old
Our fathers swept the sea,
And make the West, as they the East,
The homestead of the free.

Call To Kansas.

BY LUCY LARCOM.

Yeomen strong, hither throng!
Nature's honest men,
We will make the wilderness
Bud and bloom again.

Bring the sickle, speed the plow,
Turn the ready soil!
Freedom is the noblest pay
For the true man's toil.

Ho, brothers! come, brothers!
Hasten all with me,
We'll sing upon the Kansas plains
A song of liberty!

Father haste! o'er the waste
Lies a pleasant land;
There your fireside's altar-stones,
Fixed in truth shall stand.

There your sons, brave and good,
Shall to freemen grow,
Clustering round you, blest, at eve,
Wrong to overthrow.

Ho, brothers! come brothers!
Hasten all with me;
We'll sing etc.

Mother come! here's a home
In the waiting West,
Bring the seeds of love and peace,
You who loved them best.

Faithful hearts, lady prayers,
Keep from taint the air;
Soil a mother's tears have wet,
Golden flowers shall bear.

Come, mother! fond mother,
List, we call to thee:
We'll sing etc.

Brother brave, scan the wave!
Firm the prairie land!
Up the dark Missouri's flood
Be your canvas spread.

Sister true, join us too,
Where the Kansas flows,
Let the northern lily bloom
With the southern rose.

Brave brother, true sister!
List, we call to thee;
We'll sing etc.

One and all, hear our call,
Echo through the land!
Aid us with a willing heart,
And a strong right hand!

Feed the spark the Pilgrim struck
On old Plymouth rock!
To the watch-fires of the free
Millions glad shall flock.

Ho, brothers! come brothers!
Hasten all with me;
We'll sing etc.

PHILLIPS COUNTY CONDENSED.

Phillips county contains an area of nine hundred square miles or 576,000 acres of land. The county was organized in 1872. Population in 1873, 1,500; in 1874, 3,500. The present population

say you can "find all these in the counties comprising this land district. The past winter has been remarkably mild, and cattle have in many instances, wintered through without feed, other than that obtained by grazing. The prairie grass is of the most nutritious quality and cattle fatten upon it ready for market, without other feed. The sheep men of the county, are doing extremely well, the sheep being entirely free from disease.

Come To Kansas.

There are more than usual indications of a heavy immigration next spring to this country. Hard times at the east and poor crops, have made the people uneasy, and their eyes are turned again to the fertile and productive west. Kansas offers an inviting field for immigration. It is brim full of produce. The settler lives cheaply until he raises his own crops. Land is cheap here. Our state offers to the seeker of a good home and cheap lands, the best of climates, the richest of soils, churches, railroads, and all the equipments and adornments of an advanced civilization already provided. All these advantages, the western bound emigrant will not overlook. They should be kept constantly before his mind. Immigration is the life-blood of the commonwealth. Our eastern friends should be constantly advised of the fact, that all things considered, Kansas is the most desirable of all the western states in which to make a home.

Hon. Chas. Sumner, in the U. S. Senate, May 19, 1866, in a speech on Kansas, said:

"A few short months only have passed since this spacious mediterranean country was open only to the savage, who ran wild in its woods and prairies; and now it has already drawn to its bosom, a population of freemen larger than Athens crowded within her historic gates, when her sons under Miltiades, won liberty for mankind on the field of Marathon; more than Sparta contained when she ruled Greece, and sent forth her devoted children, quickened by a mother's benediction, 'to return with their

will repeat the story of Illinois in the race of progress, on an increased and more liberal scale. We have fifty two million acres of land. Ten years hence our real estate ought to, and we believe will, be worth eight hundred million dollars.

valued at $900,000. The value of other farm products for 1875, is estimated at $500,000.

The School System

The Music Publishers Protective Association never had to use any of the evidence gathered by Moanfeldt in the months he spent tracking down "Home on the Range." Word of his success got around, and on December 6, 1935, the lawyer for the Goodwins called it quits.

There are two interesting footnotes to the story.

While no one ever found a copy of the 1873 *Smith County Pioneer* that would have been the simple key to the entire puzzle, ten years after the controversy ended and "Home on the Range" had been reinstated in the public domain, an eagle-eyed researcher spotted an equally "hot" Kansas newspaper in the files of the Kansas State Historical Society at Topeka. This was an issue of the *Kirwin Chief* dated February 26, 1876. Printed right on the front page was the poem "Western Home" with Dr. Higley's by-line. Here is the *Chief*'s rendering of the verses, with capitalization and punctuation copied exactly:

> Oh! give me a home where the Buffalo roam,
> Where the Deer and the Antelope play;
> Where never is heard a discouraging word,
> And the sky is not clouded all day.
> > A home! A home!
> > Where the Deer and the Antelope play,
> > Where seldom is heard a discouraging word,
> > And the sky is not clouded all day.

Oh! give me land where the bright diamond sand,
Throws its light from the glittering streams,
Where glideth along the graceful white swan,
Like the maid in her heavenly dreams.
    A home! A home!

Oh! give me a gale of the Solomon vale,
Where the life streams with buoyancy flow;
Or the banks of the Beaver, where seldom if ever,
Any poisonous herbage doth grow.
    A home! A home!

How often at night, when the heavens were bright,
With the light of the twinkling stars,
Have I stood here amazed, and asked as I gazed,
If their glory exceed that of ours.
    A home! A home!

I love the wild flowers in this bright land of ours,
I love the wild curlew's shrill scream;
The bluffs and white rocks, and antelope flocks,
That graze on the mountains so green.
    A home! A home!

The air is so pure and the breezes so free,
The zephyrs so balmy and light,
That I would not exchange my home here to range,
Forever in azures so bright.
    A home! A home!

The reader will note that nowhere in Higley's verses is there the expression "home, home on the range." The final stanza, however, contains the line "I would not exchange my home here to range." In oral transmission of the words from one singer to another this apparently was convertèd to "I would not exchange my home on the range," which seems to have made it into a cowboy song and also supplied a good, solid title. The change was a great improvement, as were other changes made by other singers as the song went the rounds orally and underwent a bit of polishing prior to being captured in that San Antonio saloon by the crude recording machine of John Avery Lomax.[11]

The remaining footnote concerns Professor Lomax. In the last of his many published song collections—*Folk Song: U.S.A.*—issued in 1947 only a few months before he died at the age of eighty, he discussed "Home on the Range" with, it seems to me, just a touch of bitterness.[12] After poking fun at Dr. Higley, he speaks of reading Homer Croy's newly published book *Corn Country,* in which the author describes a visit to Smith Center and an interview with Higley's son at Shawnee, Oklahoma, where Higley passes away in 1911.[13] Then Lomax ends with this cryptic comment: "When I read Mr. Croy's story, I turned to my files. A folklorist learns to be skeptical of any story of 'ultimate origins.' There I found a letter which stated that 'Home on the Range' was sung in Texas in 1867. Where will the trail end? My guess is that it goes far back beyond Kansas and Texas, as well, into the big songbag which the folk have held in common for centuries."[14]

NOTES

1. Released by First National in 1933.

2. On page 134 of his book *Alone* (New York: G. P. Putnam's Sons, 1938) Byrd quotes from his diary for May, 1933 (exact date not given): "One of my favorite songs is 'Home on the Range.' It's the second song I've ever learned to sing (the other was 'Carry Me Back to Old Virginny' and even that I never dared to sing except in the cockpit of an airplane, where nobody could hear me). And tonight I sang while washing the dishes. Solitude hasn't mellowed my voice any, but I had great fun. A gala evening, in fact."

3. From an article written by John A. Lomax for "Fiddlin' Joe's Song Corral" in Street & Smith's *Wild West Weekly* for June 30, 1934, pp. 133–35.

4. Brunswick 137; Victor 21627.

5. The other five individuals named by the Goodwins were Hugo Frey, Oscar J. Fox, David W. Guion, James Matte, and Carson Robison.

6. After 1932 the front cover of Guion's solo arrangement carried the line "President Franklin D. Roosevelt's Favorite Song." This and other Guion arrangements of western numbers may still be obtained from G. Schirmer. Born at Ballinger, Texas, in 1892, the composer now lives in Dallas.

7. From the report of Samuel Moanfeldt to the Music Publishers Protective Association, which is included in the lengthy article "Home on the Range" by Kirke Mechem, first printed in the *Kansas Historical Quarterly*, 17 (Nov., 1949), 313–39, later issued in booklet form and still available from the Kansas State Historical Society at Topeka. Moanfeldt's report on Mrs. Giddeon appears on page 332–33.

8. Ibid., p. 333.

9. Ibid., p. 335.

10. Interview with Moanfeldt, Jan. 28, 1936.

11. Aside from Goodwin's version, at least two other variants of the Higley poem were in print prior to the publication of the words and music for "Home on the Range" by Lomax in 1910. The earliest of these consists of eight lines in *The Border and the Buffalo* by John R. Cook, originally published in 1907 (Topeka, Kans.: Crane Co.), reissued in 1938 as a Lakeside Classic (Chicago: Lakeside Press), and reprinted facsimile in 1967 by Citadel Press (New York). The following quotation recalling an incident that happened in the 1870s is from pages 413–14 of the Lakeside and Citadel editions: "Another hunter, a Prodigal Son, also composed a few verses when he was leaving western Kansas to hunt in Texas. The words were sung all over the range with as much vim as the old-time John Brown's Body. It had a very catchy tune, and with the melody from the hunters' voices it was beautiful and soul-inspiring to me. One stanza and the chorus is all that I can recall of it. It ran thus:

> I love these wild flowers, in this fair land of ours,
> I love to hear the wild curlew scream
> On the cliffs of white rock, where the antelope flock,
> To graze on the herbage so green.
> > O, give me a home where the buffalo roam,
> > Where the deer and the antelope play,
> > Where seldom is heard a discouraging word
> > And the sky is not cloudy all day."

Git Along, Little Dogies

The *Journal of American Folklore*, 22 (Apr.-June, 1909), 256–61, printed an article by G. F. Will, "Songs of the Western Cowboys," which included eight stanzas and a chorus under the title "A Home on the Range." Will could supply no information on their origin but said they were well known among cowboys in the Northwest. Except for shifting the locale from the Beaver to the Platte and the use of the expression "home on the range" in both title and text, the first six stanzas and the chorus follow the Higley pattern fairly closely. Stanzas 7 and 8, quoted below, are strangers.

> The prairie all checkered with buffalo paths,
> Where once they roamed proudly to and fro;
> But now they've grown dim where the hunters have been,
> And the cowboys have laid them so low.
>
> The red-men pressed in these parts of the West
> And likely they never will return,
> For the farmers they start in search of these parts
> Whenever the story they learn.

12. John A. Lomax and Alan Lomax, *Folk Song: U.S.A.* (New York: Duell, Sloan and Pearce, 1947), pp. 197–98.

13. Homer Croy, *Corn Country* (New York: Duell, Sloan and Pearce, 1947), chap. 20, "The Amazing Story of 'Home on the Range,'" pp. 164–80.

14. Lomax, *Folk Song: U.S.A.*, p. 198.

15

"The Little Old Sod Shanty
on the Claim"

Like the cowboy, the sod-busting homesteader of the western prairies produced a sheaf of colorful songs to embellish his own special page in the book of American frontier history. Here is one of his best, the words written by some lonely bachelor who is generally believed to have fitted his verses to the tune of a popular song of the day, "The Little Old Cabin in the Lane." Composed in 1871 by William Shakespeare Hays, the older song included the following lines:

> De hinges dey got rusted an' de door has tumbled down,
> And de roof lets in de sunshine an' de rain,
> An' de only friend I've got now is dis good ole dog ob mine,
> In de little old log cabin in de lane.

A contemporary of still-remembered songwriter Henry C. Work ("Grandfather's Clock," "Kingdom Coming," "Marching through Georgia"), Hays moonlighted as a tunesmith while working for a newspaper in his native Louisville, Kentucky. Sigmund Spaeth, in *A History of Popular Music in America*, says that Hays composed more than three hundred songs, many of them of the pseudo-Negro type popularized by his more able predecessor Stephen Foster, and ranked as the most popular composer of his time.[1] But he is virtually forgotten today.

In the Spring, 1973, issue of the *Journal of the Folklore Society of Greater Washington*, folksong buff Frank Goodwyn points out that "The Little Old Sod Shanty on the Claim" was not the first parody of Will Hays's "The Little Old Cabin in the Lane," written in 1871. Just four years later, in 1875, an obvious imitation was published in sheet

A rank amateur at building must have knocked together this "little old sod shanty" photographed in Comanche County, Kansas, during the 1880s. The gallused owner will be lucky if it holds together until he proves up on his claim. He is taking his ease behind a wire fence that serves as a handy clothesline. One look at the treeless prairie in the background and there is no need to ask why early homesteaders built with sod. Courtesy of the Kansas State Historical Society, Topeka.

music with the title "The Old Log Cabin in the Lane." Words were by Grace Carlton, music by J. C. Chamberlain. The chorus:

> Ah, yes, I am old and feeble now, my head is bending low,
> And I never more shall hoe the corn again.
> Yet the angels they will lead me, when my time has come to go,
> From my little old log cabin in the lane.

As the words follow the same pattern as the Hays composition and the melody is not too different (but different enough to avoid infringing the copyright), our lonely bachelor homesteader could well have used either song as a model.[2]

The words of "The Little Old Sod Shanty on the Claim" as given below were printed on the reverse side of a sod house photograph taken in 1885 by Jasper N. Templeman of Miller, South Dakota, and sold to tourists on early transcontinental railway trains. Files of the Nebraska State Historical Society contain a different picture of a prairie shanty with the identical verses on the back, this one issued by photographer W. R. Cross of Niobrara, Nebraska. The air is from the 1871 sheet music for Will Hays's song.

Git Along, Little Dogies

liv - ing in this way, Though my bill of fare is al - ways rath - er

tame, And I'm hap - py as a clam, —— on this

land of Un - cle Sam, In my lit - tle old sod shan - ty on the claim.

CHORUS

The hin - ges are of leath - er and the win - dows have no glass, While the

roof, it lets the howl - ing bliz - zard in. And I

hear the hun - gry coy - ote as he sneaks up through the grass 'Round the

lit - tle old sod shan - ty on the claim.

I am looking rather seedy now while holding down my claim,
And my victuals are not always served the best,
And the mice play slyly 'round me as I lay me down to sleep
In my little old sod shanty on the claim.
Yet I rather like the novelty of living in this way,
Though my bill of fare is always rather tame,
And I'm happy as a clam, on this land of Uncle Sam,
In my little old sod shanty on the claim.

   The hinges are of leather and the windows have
     no glass,
   While the roof, it lets the howling blizzard in.

170

And I hear the hungry coyote as he sneaks up
   through the grass
'Round my little old sod shanty on the claim.

But when I left my Eastern home, so happy and so gay,
To try to win my way to wealth and fame,
I little thought I'd come down to burning twisted hay
In my little old sod shanty on the claim.
My clothes are plastered o'er with dough, and I'm
   looking like a fright,
And everything is scattered 'round the room,
And I fear if P. T. Barnum's man should get his eyes on me
He would take me from my little cabin home.[3]

I wish that some kind-hearted Miss would pity on me take
And extricate me from the mess I'm in.
The angel—how I'd bless her if thus her home she'd make
In my little old sod shanty on the claim.
And when we'd made our fortunes on these prairies of
   the West,
Just as happy as two bedbugs we'd remain,
And we'd forget our trials and our troubles as we rest
In our little old sod shanty on the plain.

And if heaven should smile upon us with now and then
   an heir
To cheer our hearts with honest pride to flame,
O, then we'd be content for the years that we have spent
In our little old sod shanty on the plain.
When time enough had 'lapsed and all those little brats
To man and honest womanhood have grown,
It won't be half so lonely when around us we shall look
And see other old sod shanties on the claim!

Who composed this down-to-earth word-portrait of a solitary man, his clothes splattered with dough, burning twisted hay to bake bread in the primitive dwelling erected on his 160 acres of free government land? In the 1938 edition of *Cowboy Songs and Other Frontier Ballads*, folksong collectors John and Alan Lomax said it was written in 1888 by Lindsey Baker of Kermit, West Virginia, after a brother returned from several years in a Kansas soddy. Readers of Louise Pound's slim volume *American Ballads and Songs* are left with the impression that this western parody on the Hays song was the work of a Nebraska homesteader, Emery Miller. The booklet *Sod House Memories*, issued in 1967 by the Sod House Society of Nebraska, credits Charles Griffiths Reynolds of Lincoln County, Nebraska. Two recent scholarly collections of western folksongs print a variant published in 1884 in a newspaper at Ashland, Kansas, presumably without *any* poet's name appended.[4]

My own files contain a forty-year-old letter from one Marjorie Collins of Milwaukee, Wisconsin, informing me that "Sod Shanty" was written by Orland Newell of Venus, Nebraska. Photographer Templeman's daughter, who in 1934 sent me the verses used above, firmly believed that her father wrote them. So it goes in the folksong business.[5]

"The Little Old Sod Shanty on the Claim" memorializes an era in western history that began when Abraham Lincoln signed the Homestead Act (1862), legislation designed to open up vast reservoirs of public lands to the people and attract farmers to sparsely settled regions of the West. Under its provisions, any male or female citizen over twenty-one, or anyone who had signified his intention of becoming a United States citizen, was permitted to file a claim on 160 acres in certain designated areas of the public domain. If he made certain improvements and lived on the homestead for five years, it became his property. A 160-acre tract, which happens to be one-quarter of a square mile, could also be obtained under an earlier act known as the Preemption Law for only a few dollars an acre, provided the preemptor improved it, lived on it for a short period, and swore it was being acquired for his own use and not for speculation. After the railroads were encouraged by huge government land grants to lay their rails across the Far West, many settlers obtained property by outright purchase from the companies.

But regardless of how they obtained their farms, most newcomers to the treeless prairie regions of the Dakotas, Nebraska, Kansas, and the Oklahoma panhandle had one common problem—how to build a house when there was virtually no wood or stone available. The axe that built the eastern frontiersman's log cabin was useless here. On many a claim there was not a tree in sight, only waist-high bluestem or buffalo grass extending to the horizon in every direction.

So what did these adventurous Americans and ambitious immigrants from northern Europe do? The settler put his ingenuity to the test and developed the sod house, taking advantage of the tough, matted roots of the natural grasses that covered the landscape. He hitched his horses or oxen to a special plow that turned over long strips of sod about a foot wide and four or five inches thick. Using a spade or axe, he chopped these into lengths he could handle and carefully piled them like bricks, but without any mortar, to form the walls of his new dwelling, walls that often were nearly three feet thick.

Door and window frames were made from old packing cases, from

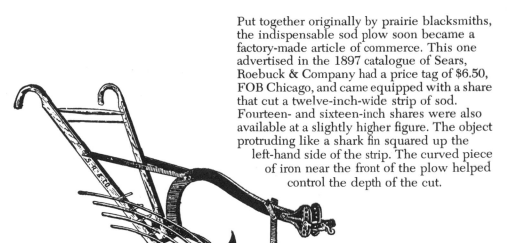

Put together originally by prairie blacksmiths, the indispensable sod plow soon became a factory-made article of commerce. This one advertised in the 1897 catalogue of Sears, Roebuck & Company had a price tag of $6.50, FOB Chicago, and came equipped with a share that cut a twelve-inch-wide strip of sod. Fourteen- and sixteen-inch shares were also available at a slightly higher figure. The object protruding like a shark fin squared up the left-hand side of the strip. The curved piece of iron near the front of the plow helped control the depth of the cut.

bought lumber if a little cash was available, or from planks laboriously sawed from a cedar or cottonwood growing in some nearby canyon. Lacking money for lumber, the settler made his roof of brush covered with clay, the whole usually topped with a layer of sod, for insulation and to anchor the roof in a gale. If he could afford a wood or shingle roof, he still topped it with sod. If windows came too dear, burlap sacking was hung over the openings until, hopefully, better times arrived. Pieces of old leather belting many a time substituted as door hinges.

When our homesteader sang of "burning twisted hay" he was only describing one of the facts of life in a soddy. With trees so scarce, firewood usually was out of the question. Special hay-burning stoves were available, and there were large metal drums that could be attached to a conventional cookstove. In summer a small amount of hay packed loosely into the drum would supply enough heat for cooking a meal without heating up the entire house. During cold weather a tightly packed drum of hay would burn all night. Of necessity, cow chips and corncobs were other popular forms of fuel.

A house with walls three feet thick and a layer of sod on the roof was said to have been cool in summer and fairly easy to heat in winter. No matter how hard the wind blew, there was little chance the house would ever tumble over. Being made largely of earth, it came close to being fireproof, which was a comfort if the prairie ever caught fire during a dry spell.

On the whole, though, sod house living was not for the squeamish. Spiders and dirt were forever dropping from the ceiling and walls. The tiniest crack in a wall was an invitation for an enterprising mouse, or

From the visible evidence, the occupants of the sod shanty in this photograph from the A. A. Forbes Collection at the University of Oklahoma obviously are finding prairie living no bed of roses. While their roof has no eaves to catch the wind, it also has very little pitch and probably caught plenty of water during spring rains. The window and door have been set flush with the inside walls, then the space around the openings plastered to reflect sunlight to the gloomy interior. Courtesy of Western History Collections, University of Oklahoma Library.

The four daughters of Nebraska pioneer Joseph M. Chrisman pose in 1886 for their neighbor, photographer Solomon D. Butcher, before the sod shanty built in northern Custer County for homesteading Elizabeth Chrisman (second from left) by her father and brothers. Homesteads were also eventually filed on by Harriette (at the far left) and by Lucie (in the square-checked dress). By the time Jennie (at the right) became of age, all the good land in their part of Custer County was taken. Elizabeth's shanty probably has a window in one of the walls away from the camera. Photograph from the Nebraska State Historical Society.

worse, a rattlesnake, to set up housekeeping. But in spite of it all, thousands of soddies once dotted the plains of the West and served their purpose until improvements in transportation made more conventional building materials plentiful and cheap.

Sod houses are still to be seen in Nebraska, provided one knows just where to look. A few serve as dwellings, others as storage sheds or chicken houses. However, most of those inhabited by humans have been plastered over on the outside and have had modern roofs installed, which makes them very difficult for a stranger to spot.[6]

Western Canada also had its share of homesteaders and soddies. In *Folk Songs of Canada*, editors Edith Fowke and Richard Johnston say the Dominion's prairie pioneers also sang "The Little Old Sod Shanty on the Claim." For the line

> And I'm happy as a clam on the land of Uncle Sam

the homesteading Canadian bachelor, no doubt with tongue in cheek, substituted the following:

> Oh, I'm happy as can be, for I'm single and I'm free,
> In my little old sod shanty on the claim.[7]

NOTES

1. Sigmund Spaeth, *A History of Popular Music in America* (New York: Random House, 1948), p. 158.

2. I am indebted to Joseph Hickerson at the Library of Congress for making available copies of both songs.

3. P. T. Barnum was the famous showman and circus tycoon who made a great success of exhibiting freaks such as General Tom Thumb and the Siamese Twins. Our bachelor homesteader, his clothes covered with dough from an attempt to make bread, felt that he might qualify.

4. John A. Lomax and Alan Lomax, *Cowboy Songs and Other Frontier Ballads*, rev. and enl. (New York: Macmillan Co., 1938), p. 405; Louise Pound, *American Ballads and Songs* (New York: Charles Scribner's Sons, 1922), p. 253. *Sod House Memories* was copyrighted in 1967 by Frances Jacobs Alberts of Hastings; the claim for authorship of the poem (p. 66) was made by Reynolds's daughter, Mrs. George H. Alexander of Omaha. The variant from the *Clark County Clipper* (Ashland, Kans.), Sept. 25, 1884, is reprinted in Richard E. Lingenfelter, Richard A. Dwyer, and David Cohen, *Songs of the American West* (Berkeley and Los Angeles: University of California Press, 1968), p. 465, and in Austin E. Fife and Alta S. Fife, *Cowboy and Western Songs: A Comprehensive Anthology* (New York: Clarkson N. Potter, 1969), p. 68.

5. In addition to having had numerous alleged creators, this song also had an abundance of progeny, so to speak. "The family of songs sired by 'The Little Old Sod Shanty' is as numerous and varied as the folks at a Mormon family reunion," say Austin and Alta Fife in *Cowboy and Western Songs*. "There are little vine-clad cottages, little *adobe casas*, log cabins, and dugouts. There are answers to 'The Little Old Sod Shanty,' and answers to the answers" (p. 67). On the pages in their book which follow these comments the Fifes present half a dozen interesting parodies. A few additional variants on the same theme may be found in chapter 7 of their earlier book *Songs of the Cowboys, by N. Howard ("Jack") Thorp* (New York: Clarkson N. Potter, Bramhall House, 1966).

6. An excellent source of information on the soddy is *Sod Walls: The Story of the Nebraska Sod House*, by Roger L. Welsch, a professor of folklore and English at the University of Nebraska, Lincoln. Published in 1968 by Purcell's (Broken Bow, Nebr.), the book is lavishly illustrated with photographs, most of them taken in the 1880s, from the famous Solomon D. Butcher collection at the Nebraska State Historical Society, Lincoln.

7. Edith Fowke and Richard Johnston, *Folk Songs of Canada* (Waterloo, Ontario: Waterloo Music Co., 1954), p. 91.

16

"Great Grandad"

Not all of our western folksongs had their origin among dwellers on the western prairies. "Great Grandad," which is found in many elementary school books and was used freely by Aaron Copland in the opening scene of his ballet *Billy the Kid*, began its career on the pages of the *Saturday Evening Post* for February 28, 1925.

The original poem, titled "Great Grandad," was the work of Lowell Otus Reese, a California journalist who published considerable light verse, virtually all of which has long since been forgotten. The poem from the *Post* probably would have suffered the same fate but for an imaginative and musically inclined rancher named Romaine Lowdermilk, whose dogies grazed beside the usually dry Hassayampa River near Wickenburg, Arizona. Lowdermilk also wrote western yarns for the now-defunct pulp magazines. In his spare hours he liked to sing and strum a guitar.

At about the time "Great Grandad" first appeared in print, Lowdermilk became a "dude rancher," a business in which musical talent is as great an asset as the ability to rope a cow or brand a calf. Being a subscriber to the *Post*, he spotted the Reese poem, worked up a sprightly tune, and soon was entertaining his guests with the exploits of the stalwart old gentleman who helped tame the frontier while keeping twenty-one sons in line.

Before long, other singing dude wranglers throughout the Southwest were adding "Great Grandad" to their repertoires. Reese's name was soon forgotten as the humorous tale went the rounds by word of mouth, and "Great Grandad" passed into what the folklore experts call oral tradition. Furthermore, each entertainer who adopted it added or

"Great Grandad"

He was a citizen tough and grim,
Danger was duck-soup to him.

Artist Aldren A. Watson's conception of that no-nonsense pioneer, Great Grandad, from *Cowboy Jamboree: Western Songs and Lore*, collected and told by Harold W. Felton. Copyright 1951 by Alfred A. Knopf, Inc. Reprinted by permission of the publisher.

changed a little here and there, which accounts for the many variants of the song in print today. One of the most original additions is to be found in the Frank C. Brown collection of North Carolina folklore. This note of optimism was contributed by Obadiah Johnson of Crossnore, North Carolina:

> Grandad died at eighty-nine;
> Twenty-one boys he left behind.
> Times have changed, but you never can tell;
> You might yet do half as well.[1]

The first time "Great Grandad" appeared on the pages of a songbook was in 1929. Eight stanzas were published in the folio *The Lonesome Cowboy*, which I compiled. Reese's name was not indicated because I had no clue as to the source of the lyrics. In the same year the first recording was made—a 78 I cut for the American Record Corporation. For reasons known only to the company, this recording of "Gran-

177

One *had* to be "tough and grim" to eke out a living in Custer County, Nebraska, where this photograph was taken by Solomon D. Butcher in 1887. On the other hand, judging by the antlers on the roof, the hunting must have been good, and Great Grandad's soddy has a shady patio air-conditioned by nature's breezes. Note the two bird cages. Photograph from the Library of Congress.

dad" was issued under a number of pseudonyms—Whitey Johns, Jimmie Price, the Lone Star Ranger—but anyone making a comparison will find that these shadowy characters all have the same voice.[2] Because the song was a bit short for a ten-inch disc, it was necessary to stretch it out. So, before I faced the microphone, I went off in a corner and dreamed up four lines to introduce the ten stanzas more or less by Reese. These are the lines beginning "I have a little song" in the version which follows.

Great Gran - dad, when the West was young, He
barred his door with a wag - on tongue, For the
times was hard and the red - skins mocked, And he
said his prayers with a shot - gun cocked.

I have a little song I'll sing to you;
'Tain't particularly old, 'tain't particularly new;
'Tain't particularly funny, 'tain't particularly sad,
Just a song about my Great Grandad.

Great Grandad, when the West was young,
He barred his door with a wagon tongue,
For the times was hard and the redskins mocked,
And he said his prayers with a shotgun cocked.

He was a citizen tough and grim,
Danger was duck-soup to him.
He ate cornpone and bacon fat,
When his great grandson would starve on that.

Great Grandad was a busy man;
He cooked his grub in a frying pan,
Picked his teeth with a hunting knife,
And he wore the same suit all his life.

Twenty-one children came to bless
The old man's home in the wilderness,
But Great Grandad he didn't lose heart,
His dogs hunted rabbits and they ketched right smart.

Twenty-one boys, and how they grew
Tall and strong on the bacon, too.
They slept on the floor with the dogs and cats,
And hunted in the woods for their coonskin hats.

Twenty-one boys, and not one bad;
They didn't get fresh with old Grandad;
For if they had, he'd have been right glad
To tan their hides with a hickory gad.

He raised 'em rough but he raised 'em well,
And if their heads began to swell
He filled 'em full of the fear of God
And he straightened 'em up with an old ramrod.

They grew strong of heart and hand.
A firm foundation for our land;
Twenty-one boys, but his great grandson
He has a terrible time with one.

Great Grandad was gaunt with toil,
His face was lined by the sun and soil.
Great grandson is slick and clean
And he rides to work in his limousine.

Great grandson now falls asleep
And he fears no harm in the darkness deep,
For Great Grandad has fought and won
And made the land safe for his great grandson.[3]

In 1931, "Great Grandad" appeared in a second printed collection, published by Alfred A. Knopf, called *Singing Cowboy*, compiled by folklorist Margaret Larkin, who had been exposed to the song in the Southwest. John and Alan Lomax found it interesting and included it in the revised, enlarged edition of *Cowboy Songs and Other Frontier Ballads*, first issued by Macmillan in 1938 and reprinted many times since. In 1966, musicologist Charles Haywood selected it as one of five English-language folk tunes from the United States for his *Folk Songs of the World*, published by the John Day Company.

In addition to the songbooks mentioned above, I have seen at least two dozen others with "Great Grandad," several of them printed in Canada. Naturally, no editor who used the song had ever heard of poet Lowell Otus Reese. But it must be admitted, as a matter of fact, it was not until 1966 that I myself learned Reese was the author of the

Lowell Otus Reese (1866–1948). Photograph courtesy of California State Library.

amusing lyrics I borrowed from Romaine Lowdermilk almost fifty years ago and have been singing ever since.

Lowell Otus Reese was an Indiana farm boy who moved to California in 1894 at the age of twenty-eight, tried teaching and prospecting, and in 1900 went to work for the Los Angeles *Times*. From then until his death in 1948 at Oakland, California, he wrote almost continuously for newspapers and magazines.

Another Reese poem, one also launched by the *Saturday Evening Post*, has managed to survive. This is "Snagtooth Sal," whose setting is Laramie. The words were printed and credited to Reese in the second John Lomax anthology, *Songs of the Cattle Trail and Cow Camp*, brought out in 1919 by the Macmillan Company. In 1929 "Sal" appeared "as Sung by Henry Jason Bolles" and with piano accompaniment in a song collection by Frank Shay, *Drawn from the Wood* (Macaulay Company, New York). Reese's name was nowhere to be seen. John and Alan Lomax put things to rights by picking up the Shay melody and giving Reese a credit line when, in 1934, they issued *American Ballads and Folk Songs* (Macmillan). But the poor poet was left out in the cold once more in 1969 when Austin and Alta Fife brought out their monumental work *Cowboy and Western Songs*. There the headnote reads: "Melody: Capitol P-8332, Roger Wagner Chorale. Text: Gordon 675."[4]

NOTES

An earlier version of this chapter appeared under the title " 'Great Grandad': The Story of a Song" in *Music Educators Journal*, 55, no. 7 (Mar., 1969), 56–57.

1. *The Frank C. Brown Collection of North Carolina Folklore*, vol. 2, *Folk Ballads from North Carolina*, ed. Henry M. Belden and Arthur Palmer Hudson (Durham, N.C.: Duke University Press, 1952), p. 621.
2. See the discography in Appendix B.
3. The tune given here is from John White and George Shackley, *The Lonesome Cowboy: Songs of the Plains and Hills* (New York: Al Piantadosi, 1929), pp. 17–18; the text is from my 78 of the song.
4. The verses of "Snagtooth Sal" were scattered in Lowell Otus Reese's short story "The Constable of Copper Sky" in the *Saturday Evening Post* for March 31, 1917 (p. 10ff.); this story was reprinted in the Reese anthology *Little Injun* (New York: Thomas Y. Crowell Co., 1927), pp. 34–61. John A. Lomax, *Songs of the Cattle Trail and Cow Camp* (New York: Macmillan Co., 1919), pp. 69–70; Frank Shay, *Drawn from the Wood* (New York: Macaulay Co., 1929), pp. 120–23; John A. Lomax and Alan Lomax, *American Ballads and Folk Songs* (New York: Macmillan Co., 1934), pp. 405–6; Austin E. Fife and Alta S. Fife, *Cowboy and Western Songs: A Comprehensive Anthology* (New York: Clarkson N. Potter, 1969), p. 288.

17

"Great Grandma"

During the National Folk Festival at Denver in May, 1966, Ben Gray Lumpkin of the University of Colorado called my attention to the October, 1962, number of *Western Folklore* (21, no. 4), which carried the article "American Cowboy and Western Pioneer Songs in Canada" by Edith Fowke of Toronto. Mrs. Fowke makes the following statement: "More recently Kenneth Peacock found in Newfoundland a version of 'Great Grandma,' a pioneer song dating from the days of the California gold rush."[1] I have news for Mrs. Fowke, Mr. Peacock, and anyone else who may have been under the impression that "Great Grandma" is of such ancient vintage. Actually the old gal is only forty-odd years old. I should know, because I happen to be her father.

From the end of 1926 through 1936 I was a moonlighting singer of western ballads from New York radio stations, using the name "Lonesome Cowboy," although I was neither lonesome nor a cowboy. Whenever I could spare a few hours from my daytime job with a map company, I also made records (singles) for the American Record Corporation, twenty sides in all.[2]

One of my most popular broadcast numbers, judging by the fan mail we radio singers used to receive in those days, was a humorous ditty known as "Great Grandad" that I obtained from Romaine Lowdermilk, Arizona dude rancher, author, and entertainer.[3] Many years later I learned it was based on a poem by Lowell Otus Reese from the *Saturday Evening Post* for February 28, 1925. I have always understood that Romaine supplied the tune for this colorful account of the tribulations of a pioneer with twenty-one sons, which usually begins:

> Great Grandad when the West was young,
> Barred his door with a wagon tongue,
> For the times was rough and the redskins mocked,
> And he said his prayers with his shotgun cocked.[4]

After I had sung about this stalwart old gentleman many times, it occurred to me that someone should do something for his helpmate. After all, Great Grandma also had stood up nobly to the hardships of life on the frontier, not to mention all those children. So I composed the following four stanzas:

> Great Grandma, when the West was new,
> Wore hoop skirts and a bustle, too;
> But when the Injuns came and things looked bad,
> She fit right alongside of Great Grandad.
>
> She worked hard seven days in the week
> To keep Grandad well fed and sleek;
> She b'iled the beans and she hung out the wash,
> And she never had time to drink tea, by gosh.
>
> Twenty one necks she had to scrub,
> Wash twenty-one shirts in the old wash tub,
> Cook twenty-one meals three times a day;
> No wonder Grandma's hair turned gray.
>
> She worked all day, and she slept all night,
> Which, it seems to me, is just about right;
> With great grandaughter it's the other way,
> She's up all night and she sleeps all day.

Either because I was overly modest or because I suspected my effort at verse making was a bit amateurish, the first time I tried "Great Grandma" out on the air, singing it to the same tune as "Great Grandad," I said the verses had been sent to me by an anonymous radio listener. Shortly thereafter, in 1929, in collaboration with a fellow performer at station WOR, I published a soft-cover book, *The Lonesome Cowboy*. It included both "Great Grandad" and "Great Grandma." In this I still did not take credit for having composed the above four stanzas, which now seem to have become part of the western tradition.[5]

In 1933 "Great Grandad" and "Great Grandma" turned up in the book *Cowboy Lore* by Jules Verne Allen, working New Mexico cowboy and Victor recording artist. Accompanying the two songs was this editorial comment: "Although I have been singing the Great Grandad song I do not know the author of either 'Great Grandad' or 'Great Grandma'. I have even added verse number nine to Grandad myself. Whoever the author may be, he or she, more power to them. I think

She b'iled the beans and she hung out the wash
And she never had time to drink tea, by gosh.

With assists from several minor "poets," Great Grandma carved out her own niche in the Western Folklore Hall of Fame. She is depicted here by Aldren A. Watson, illustrator of *Cowboy Jamboree: Western Songs and Lore*, collected and told by Harold W. Felton. Copyright 1951 by Alfred A. Knopf, Inc. Reprinted by permission of the publisher.

these are great songs. If I knew the author, due credit would be given." [6] On reading this, I immediately wrote Jules, telling what I knew of the history of "Great Grandad" and confessing that "Great Grandma" was my own offspring. I never received an acknowledgment of my letter.

That was the last I heard of my brainchild until recently when I retired from business and again found time for an active interest in western balladry. In my local library, I ran across *Americans and Their Songs* by Frank Luther. Frank had started singing for the radio and making records at about the same time I did but has stayed in the music field all his life. To my surprise, his book, published in 1942, contains not only "Great Grandad" but "Great Grandma" stretched out to eleven stanzas. My baby had grown up. My original four stanzas were virtually intact and were dropped into the song at convenient spots. I also learned that in 1950 Frank Luther had put his "Great Grandma" on a long-playing record—*Get Along Little Dogies* (Decca DL 5035)—along with "Great Grandad" and twenty other songs of the West. I had recorded only "Great Grandad," in 1929. Frank Luther is a very busy man who probably has forgotten more songs that I ever knew. Recently, when I located him in New York, where he is occupied with producing educational records, and talked with him about "Great Grandma," he was unable to recall where he had obtained the following version included in *Americans and Their Songs* back in 1942:

Back in the days of forty-nine
Great grandma was in her prime;
She packed up her things and the kids right glad,
And headed for the West with great grandad.

They joined up with a wagon train
And prodded that ox-team across the plain,
Nothin' to see but sage and sand,
Not one hitch-hiker nor a hot dog stand.

One fine day they heard a meadow lark,
Great grandad says, "Here's where we park."
Great grandma says, "Well, I'm game";
Unloaded the kids and they staked out a claim.

Great grandad built a house of sod
By a hustle and tussle and the grace of God;
Just as he was finishin' the roof
A cyclone came and the house went "poof."

They had a team of buckskin mules,
Great grandma tried to drive the fools;
They ran away with a load of kraut,
Upset the buckboard 'n threw her out.

Great grandma, when the West was new,
Wore hoop skirts and a bustle too;
But when the Injuns came and things looked bad
She fit right alongside o' great grandad.

She worked hard seven days in the week
To keep grandad well fed and sleek;
She b'iled the beans and she hung out the wash
And she never had time to drink tea, by gosh.

She could ride herd and plow the shoot
Boss great grandad and the kids to boot
And the kids they had; in just a few years
There was twenty-one boys as wild as steers.

Twenty-one boys a-raisin' Cain,
Chasin' each other across the plain;
Great grandma was proud, no doubt,
But she had to work like all get out.

Twenty-one necks she had to scrub;
Wash twenty-one shirts in the old wash tub;
Twenty-one meals three times a day—
That's how she fritter'd her time away!

She work'd all day and slept all night
And it seems to me that's just about right
But her great grandaughter's just the other way;
She's up all night and she sleeps all day.[7]

Although in his explanatory notes Frank tried to make it clear that the above stanzas are of recent origin, they unfortunately are indexed under the heading "Songs of the Forty-niners" and are located in the book among a number of items that do go back more than a century, for example, "Sweet Betsy from Pike" and "Joe Bowers." Consequently, a bit of confusion on the part of Canadian folksong collectors is understandable. At any rate, Frank Luther is happy that he, too, could contribute his bit to the folklore of North America.

The version of the song called "Old Grandma" which Kenneth Peacock heard in Newfoundland is printed in *Folk Songs of Canada* by Edith Fowke and Richard Johnston. Its tune is quite different from that used widely throughout the United States for "Great Grandad" and "Great Grandma," and it appears to have been put together by a singer unfamiliar with either Frank Luther's book or his record. A close examination reveals that this eight-stanza variant includes fourteen lines from my own original sixteen quoted above. Combined with these are ten lines from "Great Grandad" and the following two strangers:

Great Grandma had a broody hen;
She got it from her cousin Ben.
In a pair of pants she made a nest,
And the hen hatched out a coat and vest.

She could make good mountain dew,
Home-baked beans and Irish stew.
Great Grandpa once he skinned a goat,
And Great Grandma made a new fur coat.[8]

NOTES

An earlier version of this chapter appeared in *Western Folklore*, 27 (Jan., 1968), 27–31.

1. This version of "Great Grandma" appears in *Folk Songs of Canada* by Edith Fowke and Richard Johnston (Waterloo, Ontario: Waterloo Music Co., 1954), pp. 94–95.
2. Only three of my recordings carried my own name—"Whoopee Ti Yi Yo, Git Along Little Dogies" and two versions of "The Strawberry Roan." See the introduction, "Just for the Record," for the full story, also the discography in Appendix B.

3. For more on Lowdermilk see chapter 9.

4. For the history of "Great Grandad" see chapter 16.

5. John White and George Shackley, *The Lonesome Cowboy: Songs of the Plains and Hills* (New York: Al Piantadosi, 1929); "Great Grandad," quoted above, appears on pages 17–18, "Great Grandma" on page 19.

6. Jules Verne Allen, *Cowboy Lore* (San Antonio: Naylor Printing Co., 1933), p. 127. Allen's statement about his having added verse 9 to "Great Grandad" is erroneous. A comparison with the original in the *Saturday Evening Post* shows that Lowell Otus Reese wrote all nine stanzas printed in *Cowboy Lore*.

7. Frank Luther, *Americans and Their Songs* (New York and London: Harper & Brothers, 1942), pp. 129–30.

8. Fowke, *Folk Songs of Canada*, p. 95.

18

Carl T. Sprague, Singing Cowboy

All day long on the prairies I ride,
Not even a dog to trot by my side.
My fire I kindle from chips gathered 'round,
My coffee I boil without being ground.
I wash in a pool and I dry on a sack,
I carry my wardrobe all on my back.[1]

When white-haired Carl T. "Doc" Sprague strums his antique guitar and lets go with this musical description of the self-reliant, old-time cowhand cooking over a cow-chip fire and uncomplainingly doing his thing for "forty a month and found," it takes him back half a century to the days when his voice was heard throughout the land, singing his songs of the West. As early as 1925 Victor was issuing discs bearing Carl's name, thereby establishing him as one of the very first—on recordings, at least—of America's numerous "singing cowboys."

Born near Houston, Texas, in 1895 and raised in a family of cattlemen, Carl recalls that he learned most of his songs at roundup campfires. "My uncles and I," he says, "used to sit around the fire at night and sing the very same songs that cowboys sang many years before. I used to go on cattle drives with them, and we'd make camp right there on the open prairie where there wasn't anything but cattle, horses, and stars. That was where I learned my songs, from real cowboys."[2]

A phenomenally successful phonograph record—"The Prisoner's Song," made by Vernon Dalhart, another Texas-born singer—inspired Sprague to try getting his own large collection of homespun ballads

Carl T. Sprague in 1925, when he made his
first recordings of cowboy songs for Victor.

onto discs. So in the summer of 1925, while on vacation from his work with the athletic staff of Texas A & M College, he packed up his "git fiddle" and invaded Victor's studios at Camden, New Jersey. There he succeeded in putting ten of his songs, half of them cowboy numbers, "on wax," as they used to say in the recording business. Only six were released—on the now old-fashioned 78 rpm platters—among them "When the Work's All Done This Fall," the touching story of a cowhand killed in a night stampede, unfortunately a fairly common occurrence in the era of the open range. This proved to be the most popular of Carl's recordings. More than nine hundred thousand copies were sold, a terrifically high score in those days, especially for an unknown singer.

In 1965 Carl felt greatly honored when this same ballad, "When the Work's All Done This Fall," and three of his other favorites were reissued on a long-playing disc in RCA Victor's Vintage series, *Authentic Cowboys and Their Western Folksongs* (LPV 522). The other songs were "Utah Carroll," "Following the Cow Trail" (often titled "The Trail to Mexico"), and "The Mormon Cowboy." The first three may be found in the anthology *Cowboy Songs and Other Frontier Ballads* by John Avery Lomax, first issued in 1910, revised and enlarged in 1938, and still very much in print. "The Mormon Cowboy" is a musical description of a hoedown at Globe, Arizona, sent to Carl years ago by one of his fans.

Carl matriculated at Texas A & M in 1915. College was interrupted by a two-year hitch in the aviation section of the Signal Corps, which took him to France. Back home again, Carl returned to Texas A & M, intending eventually to become a rancher. But on graduation, in 1922, he was persuaded by head coach D. X. Bible to join the athletic department, where he remained for fifteen years. In 1925, backed by a group of student musicians, he did a bit of musical moonlighting with an hour-long, once-a-week program from the campus experimental radio station, WTAW. His band, the Campus Cats, was composed of violins, guitars, banjos, trumpet, saxophone, and a trombone.

When his 1925 recording session at Camden proved a success, Carl decided to go east again in 1926, following his marriage to Laura Bess Mayo of Fairfield, a graduate of Sam Houston College and the University of Texas. On this second trip to Camden, which produced six recordings, Carl not only had his bride with him but, feeling that violins would give variety to his recordings, took along two of his Texas Aggie musician friends—Charles R. Dockum and Harold J. McKenzie. In 1927 six more recordings were made for Victor at Savannah, Georgia, a final half dozen at Dallas in 1929.[3]

In those rough-and-ready days of the young phonograph record industry a cowboy singer ordinarily received no royalties on his discs, just a flat fee of seventy-five dollars per side, unless he had written the song or in some way contributed substantially to the final result beside the mere fact of singing it. Carl recalls that he was able to collect a half-cent royalty on about half of his two dozen numbers, which he considered a handsome boost for a young fellow just starting married life. For his first and most popular record, "When the Work's All Done This Fall," he put his own touches on the tune and thus qualified for both the seventy-five-dollar fee and the royalty.

Carl's favorite songs today are the one just mentioned and three others with a religious connotation—"The Last Great Roundup," "Rounded Up in Glory," and "The Cowboy's Dream." The last named is another famous ditty which, as rendered by Carl Sprague, has this opening stanza:

> Last night as I lay on the prairie
> And looked at the stars in the sky,
> I wondered if ever a cowboy
> Would drift to that sweet by-and-by.
> I know there is many a stray cowboy
> Who'll be lost at that great final sale,
> When he might have gone into green pastures
> Had he known of the dim narrow trail.[4]

Established for some years now at Bryan, Texas, near his old college, Carl still enjoys singing and accompanying himself on a forty-five-year-old guitar. He performs occasionally for local television stations, appears at folk festivals, and is in demand for home talent shows. In recent years he has been enticed as far afield as the University of California at Los Angeles and the University of Illinois to bring to interested groups his western songs and his comments on the cowboy's contribution to America's musical heritage.

Carl never continued a musical career, except for fun. After leaving the athletic staff at Texas A & M, he operated a combination filling station and grocery store for four years, then became a traveling life insurance salesman. Having remained in the army reserve, in a cavalry unit, when World War II came he returned to active duty and served six years on recruiting and induction work at Houston and Dallas. When he finished his service, with the rank of major, he could look back with pride on thirty-three years with the colors.

Following his last six years in uniform, Carl served for three years with the Veterans' Administration at Dallas before going back to selling insurance to Texas Aggies. He also employed his sales talents marketing cemetery lots. Today he is fully retired from just about

Carl Sprague's guitar has a metal disc inside to give added volume when needed. Photograph by Gene Dennis, Bryan, Texas, *Eagle*.

everything, he says, except a little hunting and fishing and helping friends with one of his specialties—pecan grafting. He also continues to lead the singing at the Bryan Lions Club and at the businessmen's Bible class at the First Baptist Church Sunday school.

Much to his surprise, in 1972 Carl again found himself in the recording business. At the request of Richard Weize of Harmenhausen, West Germany, an enthusiast for things western, Carl taped fourteen songs for an LP released in the fall of that year on the German label Folk Variety, *Carl T. Sprague: The First Popular Singing Cowboy* (FV 12001).

Carl Sprague's first and most popular recording was "When the Work's All Done This Fall." Like many another famous cowboy ballad, it evolved from a poem first printed in a newspaper—in this case verses written by Montana cowboy D. J. O'Malley for the October 6, 1893, issue of the Miles City *Stock Growers' Journal.* O'Malley titled his verses "After the Roundup" and wrote them to fit the tune of the 1892 waltz-time song hit "After the Ball" by Charles Harris, still popular today. O'Malley included this chorus:

> After the roundup's over,
> After the shipping's done,
> I'm going straight back home, boys,
> Ere all my money's gone.
> My mother's dear heart is breaking,
> Breaking for me, that's all;
> But, with God's help I'll see her,
> When work is done this fall.

Here are the words and melody from Carl's 1925 recording:

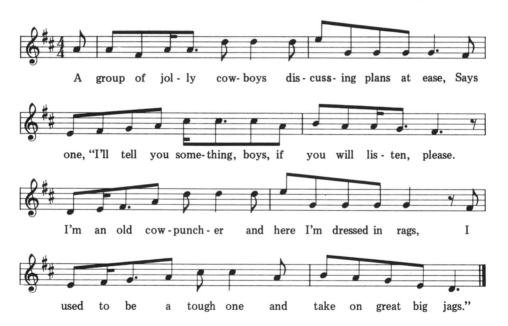

A group of jolly cowboys discussing plans at ease,
Says one, "I'll tell you something, boys, if you will listen, please.
I'm an old cowpuncher and here I'm dressed in rags,
I used to be a tough one and take on great big jags.

"But I have a home, boys, a good one, you all know,
Although I have not seen it since long, long ago.
But I'm going back to Dixie once more to see them all;
Yes, I'm going back to see my mother when the work's all done this fall.

"When I left home, boys, my mother for me cried,
She begged me not to leave her, for me she would have died.
My mother's heart is breaking, breaking for me, that's all,
And with God's help I'll see her when the work's all done this fall."

That very night this cowboy went out to stand his guard;
The night was dark and cloudy and storming very hard.
The cattle all got frightened and rushed in wild stampede;
The cowboy tried to head them while riding at full speed.

While riding in the darkness so loudly did he shout,
Trying his best to head them and turn the herd about;
His saddle horse did stumble and upon him did fall;
The boy won't see his mother when the work's all done this fall.

"Boys, send my mother my wages, the wages I have earned,
For I'm afraid, boys, my last steer I have turned.
I'm going to a new range, I hear the Master's call,
And I'll not see my mother when the work's all done this fall.

"George, you may have my saddle; Bill, you may have my bed;
Jack, you may have my pistol, after I am dead.
But think of me kindly as you look upon them all,
For I'll not see my mother when the work's all done this fall."

Poor Charlie was buried at sunrise, no tombstone at his head,
Nothing but a little slab, and this is what it said:
"Charlie died at daybreak, he died from a fall,
And he'll not see his mother when the work's all done this fall."[5]

NOTES

An earlier version of this chapter appeared in the *John Edwards Memorial Foundation Quarterly*, 6 (Spring, 1970), 32–34.

1. From "The Cowboy" (Victor 21402), sung by Carl T. Sprague. A full text appears in Clifford P. Westermeier, *Trailing the Cowboy* (Caldwell, Idaho: Caxton Printers, 1955), pp. 263–64. Titled "The Cowboy's Soliloquy," this was taken from a Trinidad, Colorado, newspaper, the *Daily Advertiser* for April 9, 1885, which credited the poem to Allen McCandless. Richard E. Lingenfelter and Richard A. Dwyer reprint this 1885 text in *Songs of the American West* (Berkeley and Los Angeles: University of California Press, 1968), pp. 342–43, with the tune from the 1910 Lomax collection, *Cowboy Songs and Other Frontier Ballads* (New York: Sturgis & Walton Co.), pp. 98–99.

2. *Eagle* (Bryan, Tex.), ca. Nov. 20, 1965.

3. See Harlan Daniel's Sprague discography in Glenn Ohrlin, *The Hell-Bound Train: A Cowboy Songbook* (Urbana: University of Illinois Press, 1973), pp. 278–80.

4. From "The Cowboy's Dream" (Victor 20122), sung by Carl T. Sprague. This song is discussed in chapter 6.

5. Victor 19747, reissued on *Authentic Cowboys and Their Western Folksongs* (RCA Victor LPV 522). O'Malley's story is told in chapter 7.

19

Two Pioneer Collectors

Although a few poems about cowpunchers were included in a perennial medicine show pamphlet, *The Life and Adventures of the American Cowboy*, first issued in 1897 by Clark Stanley, a Rhode Island purveyor of "rattlesnake oil," credit for the initial roundup of cowboy songs between the covers of a book goes to N. Howard "Jack" Thorp (1867–1940), southwestern poet, minstrel, author, and veteran cowhand. In 1908 a printshop in Estancia, New Mexico, produced 2,000 copies of Thorp's fifty-page *Songs of the Cowboys*, containing the words, and only the words, of twenty-three songs, only one of them carrying a composer's name. Among these were "Little Joe, the Wrangler," "Sam Bass," "Grand Round-up," "Educated Feller" ("Zebra Dun"), "Cow Boy's Lament," "Buffalo Range," "The Texas Cowboy," and "The Tenderfoot." Many of the songs had been gathered on a fifteen-hundred-mile ballad-collecting journey on horseback, chiefly through Texas and New Mexico, undertaken by Thorp in 1889–90.

For a revised and enlarged edition of his book, published by Houghton Mifflin in 1921, Thorp added a number of his own verses and confessed to having written "Little Joe, the Wrangler," a widely circulated ballad about a fatal accident during a night stampede. This usually is sung to the same tune as that famous prairie homesteader song "The Little Old Sod Shanty on the Claim."

Back in 1934, when I was a radio performer, I wrote Jack Thorp, asking whether he could help me locate one of the thin little booklets in a red cover that he had published in 1908 and sold all over the West for half a dollar. He was unable to help. But I did find one shortly thereafter in a secondhand bookstore and naturally consider it one of my rare treasures.

196

N. Howard "Jack" Thorp (1867–1940). The photograph was supplied by Neil M. Clark of Santa Fe, New Mexico, co-author with Thorp of the latter's posthumous autobiography, *Pardner of the Wind,* issued in 1945 by the Caxton Printers, Ltd.

In 1966 folklorists Austin and Alta Fife of Logan, Utah, made the first Thorp song collection readily available to all by incorporating a facsimile reproduction in their scholarly volume *Songs of the Cowboys, by N. Howard ("Jack") Thorp* (New York: Clarkson N. Potter, Bramhall House). The Fifes devote a chapter of discussion—often quite lengthy discussion—to each of Thorp's twenty-three songs and give many variants, parodies, and tunes. The Fife book also reprints "Banjo in the Cow Camps," an article by Thorp originally published in the *Atlantic Monthly* for August, 1940. This describes in the author's own easy-going cowboy style his experiences as a song collector, including his fifteen-hundred-mile ballad-hunting expedition on horseback that began in March of 1889 and lasted a full year.

In the introduction to Thorp's 1921 anthology *Songs of the Cowboys*, poet Alice Corbin Henderson quotes him as replying, when asked for a sketch of his life, "Just say that I've been everything but a telegraph operator or a preacher"[1]—apparently not too much of an exaggeration. Son of a well-to-do New York City lawyer, in his late teens he had to forego a college education when financial reverses overtook his father. After a spell at training polo ponies to make a living, Jack drifted to the West. He knew enough about civil engineering to become superintendent of a mine in Arizona and to become involved in a South American railroad venture. The latter proving unsuccessful, he shoveled coal on a steamer to get back to the States. He once started for the Alaska goldfields but ran out of money on the way. More than half of his life was spent in New Mexico, first as a cowboy, later as a rancher.

In addition to his two printed collections of cowboy songs, Thorp left a legacy of cattle country literature in the form of numerous magazine articles, an amusing book, *Tales of the Chuck Wagon*, published privately at Santa Fe in 1926, and *Pardner of the Wind*, a combination of autobiography, reminiscences, and examples of dry cowboy humor reflecting an intimate knowledge of New Mexico and its people over a span of forty-odd years. This was written in collaboration with Neil McCullough Clark, who still lives in Santa Fe and still writes about the West; it was issued in 1945, five years after Thorp's death, by the Caxton Printers (Caldwell, Idaho).

Another collector, to whom we owe perhaps an even greater debt for having rescued many old-time cowboy songs from oblivion, was John Avery Lomax (1867–1948), whose boyhood was spent on a farm in Bosque County, Texas, beside a branch of the Chisholm Trail. In his autobiography, *Adventures of a Ballad Hunter* (Macmillan, 1947) he tells of watching huge herds of Longhorns plodding northward, of hearing cowpunchers sing on the trail and while circling bedded-down steers at night. In his teens he began writing down the words of the songs he heard. He carried his roll of musical treasures with him when, in 1895, just before his twenty-eighth birthday, he entered the University of Texas at Austin. There he screwed up enough courage to show his songs to one of his instructors, who referred him to an eminent Ph.D. The latter bluntly told him his samples of frontier literature were "tawdry, cheap and unworthy." Crushed by this negative reaction from so exalted a personage, Lomax burned his entire collection.

John Avery Lomax (1867–1948). From a painting by J. Anthony Wills in the Lomax Memorial Room, Sid Richardson Hall, University of Texas at Austin. Courtesy of Richard T. Fleming, Curator, University Writings Collections.

An administrative post at the University of Texas followed graduation, then a job teaching freshman English at Texas A & M. In 1906 a one-year scholarship to Harvard brought Lomax east in search of a master's degree, but with cowboy songs still on his mind. On the Harvard faculty he found two kindred souls—Barrett Wendell and George Lyman Kittredge. Encouraged by them, Lomax conceived the idea of a book of such songs, and under their sponsorship he wrote the editors of a thousand newspapers in the West, describing his project and asking for help in rounding up songs of the cowboys, miners, stage drivers, freighters, and buffalo hunters. The cooperation and the response were amazing. Prominent magazines and even eastern newspapers gave their support. The result was a flood of letters that continued for years. After Lomax returned to Texas A & M, his backers at Harvard arranged for three grants of $500 each, which he used during summer vacations to travel through the West and corral more cowboy music. He carried a crude recording instrument with wax cylinders and a big horn. But as most cowboys refused to sing into the horn, the "professor," as he usually was called, often had to resort to jotting down words and tunes in the back rooms of saloons, scrawling them on envelopes while squatting near a campfire, or catching a singer behind the scenes at a rodeo. Many times a bottle of whiskey had to be used as a "loosener-upper" for an otherwise shy performer. On the whole, it was a tough assignment. To quote from Lomax: "From the beginning the cowboys who gave me songs met me with frank disbelief in my undertaking and with little respect for the intelligence of a man undertaking the work of collecting such material. But my presence created a diversion in their busy lives. They endured me without having much respect for me."[2]

With enough material in hand for a book, Lomax faced the problem of getting published. Even with a written endorsement by Theodore Roosevelt that could be printed in the front, both Appleton and Doubleday-Page turned it down. A small publishing house, Sturgis & Walton, later absorbed by Macmillan, took the gamble and in 1910 brought out *Cowboy Songs and Other Frontier Ballads*. While the book contained the words of 112 songs, the publishers felt they could afford to include only eighteen tunes from the hundred or more Lomax had been able to record by hand or on his fragile wax cylinders.

Although slow to catch on with the public, this pioneer collection, actually the first to include tunes for American folk music, eventually went through numerous printings. Somewhere along the way it was fattened by the addition of the words of forty-three more songs. It was not until 1938, however, that a new and revised edition appeared, with an air for virtually every song. Meanwhile, in 1919, material left over from *Cowboy Songs*, along with the work of a number of established western poets such as E. A. Brininstool, Henry Herbert Knibbs, Badger Clark, and James Barton Adams, filled another Lomax anthology called *Songs of the Cattle Trail and Cow Camp*. This contained no tunes, and many of the poems probably never had actually been sung by cowboys or anyone else.[3]

John Lomax broke two of the rules usually considered sacrosanct by serious ballad gatherers. First, he took the liberty of combining the best lines from the many variants he collected; second, he cleaned up, or "sanitized," some of his selections to the point where they no longer sound like the talk of rough, tough cowboys.

As to the first point, the collector himself says in his collector's note to *Cowboy Songs*: "I have violated the ethics of ballad-gatherers, in a few instances, by selecting and putting together what seemed to be the best lines from different versions, all telling the same story. Frankly, the volume is meant to be popular."[4] In short, Lomax realized his work would be wasted if the book failed to sell. Considering the difficulty he faced in getting a publisher, possibly he can be excused for having put out a readable book rather than a hodgepodge of bits and pieces from all over the West. Interested scholars can find his original material at the University of Texas.[5]

On the second count Lomax wrote: " . . . some of the strong adjectives and nouns have been softened,—Jonahed, as George Meredith would have said. There is, however, a Homeric quality about the cowboy's profanity and vulgarity that pleases rather than repulses. The broad sky under which he slept, the limitless plains over which he rode, the big, open, free life he lived near to Nature's breast, taught him simplicity, calm, directness. He spoke out plainly the impulses of his heart. But as yet so-called polite society is not quite willing to hear."[6] The reader must bear in mind that this was 1910 and quite another era in publishing, one whose "polite society" would have been aghast at today's "anything goes" attitude. It was the same era in which a Macmillan editor, when checking the manuscript of *The Virginian*, substituted a dash for Wister's five-letter word in the epithet that sparked that famous comeback "When you call me that, *smile*!"

I never was lucky enough to come by a copy of the original Lomax anthology of 1910. So during my career as a song historian I have had to be content with referring to the one in the New York Public Library. My own 1924 printing of the 1916 edition, acquired almost the minute I returned home from my memorable first visit with Romaine Lowdermilk at Wickenburg, Arizona, described in my introductory chapter, has had so much use it is virtually in shreds.

I met John Avery Lomax several times through his friend Robert W. Gordon, first head of the Archive of Folk Song at the Library of Congress, who by happenstance occupied an apartment in my parents' home at Washington, D.C. When I became interested in the work of Montana cowboy poet D. J. O'Malley (the subject of the lengthiest chapter in this book), I passed my findings on to Lomax. Later I was pleased to note that in the 1938 revised and enlarged edition of *Cowboy Songs* he gave O'Malley credit for "Charlie Rutledge," "When the Work's All Done This Fall," and "The Horse Wrangler." [7]

The last time I saw the professor from Texas was one of the unforgettable days of my life. This was January 4, 1935. The occasion was a University of Texas alumni luncheon at a New York hotel to which I had been invited by the late Tex Ritter. The attraction was the team of Lomax and Lead Belly, the latter the self-acknowledged king of the twelve-string guitar who had sung his way out of the state penitentiaries of both Texas and Louisiana.

Lomax addressed us, but, as the *Herald Tribune* put it next day, "was forced to divide his efforts between speaking to his fellow Texans and shielding his musical, murderous protege from the world of commerce. He was quite willing that Lead Belly's talents should receive proper recognition from the proper persons but, as he explained it, 'if anybody waved a $10 bill at Lead Belly he'd follow him out the door.' His chief fear was that the quick-tempered, knife-toting Negro would get loose in Harlem and win for himself another such scar as that which now girdles his neck from ear to ear."

Following lunch, the "sweet singer of the swamplands," dressed in faded farmer's overalls and strumming his battered guitar, began his amazing career as a celebrity with a two-hour recital which included "Good Night, Irene" and others of the five hundred songs Lomax said his man knew by heart. The pièce de résistance was Lead Belly's successful musical appeal to Governor Pat Neff of Texas, an appeal so touching that it had opened the prison gates and cancelled a forty-year rap for murder.

NOTES

1. N. Howard Thorp, *Songs of the Cowboys*, rev. and enl. (Boston and New York: Houghton Mifflin Co., 1921), p. xvi.

2. John A. Lomax, *Adventures of a Ballad Hunter* (New York: Macmillan Co., 1947), pp. 299–300. This autobiography was reprinted in 1971 by the Hafner Press (New York).

3. John A. Lomax, *Songs of the Cattle Trail and Cow Camp* (New York: Macmillan Co., 1919). One of the entries, Badger Clark's "A Border Affair," has become very popular in recent years as a song titled "Spanish Is the Lovin' Tongue" (see chap. 11).

4. John A. Lomax, *Cowboy Songs and Other Frontier Ballads* (New York: Sturgis & Walton Co., 1910), p. xxiii.

5. Ballad-collecting procedures of Lomax and Thorp and their views on each other's work are discussed at length by D. K. Wilgus in *Anglo-American Folksong Scholarship since 1898* (New Brunswick, N.J.: Rutgers University Press, 1959), pp. 157–65. More on the subject may be found in John O. West's article "Jack Thorp and John Lomax: Oral or Written Transmission?," *Western Folklore*, 26 (Apr., 1967), 113–18.

6. Lomax, *Cowboy Songs*, pp. xxiv–xxv.

7. "The Horse Wrangler" had appeared in Thorp's two printed collections with the title "The Tenderfoot"; in the 1921 volume Thorp credited it to Yank Hitson of Denver.

Appendix A
Where to Find More Western Songs

Cowboy music enjoyed tremendous popularity on radio, also on records, during the late 1920s and the 1930s. The vogue for listening to songs of the American West was accompanied by a flood of soft-cover folios, issued chiefly in New York and Chicago, often carrying the name and picture of a well-known performer and featuring his favorite numbers. As these ephemeral publications disappeared from the market they were replaced by the better-researched hard-cover western song collections listed below. Those classified as currently in print may be ordered through booksellers or obtained by writing directly to publishers. Prices may be determined in advance by consulting that annual publication titled *Books in Print* found in virtually every bookstore and in the reference department of many libraries. *Books in Print* includes a list of publishers' names and addresses.

Helpful data on cowboy song recordings, both present and past, will be found in the second half of this appendix.

Books Currently in Print

Songs of the American West. Richard E. Lingenfelter and Richard A. Dwyer. Music editor, David Cohen. Berkeley and Los Angeles: University of California Press, 1968. This monumental six-hundred-page work contains the words of 283 songs, both old and relatively new, each with a line of music. While the cowboy and the miner have the largest representation—about fifty songs for each—every other significant group that moved across the pages of western history is well documented in song. These include the Mormons, homesteaders, railroaders, soldiers, even the hobos.

Cowboy Songs and Other Frontier Ballads. John A. Lomax and Alan Lomax. New York: Macmillan Co., 1938. The two hundred songs in this often-reprinted collection include most of those in the earlier Lomax anthology bearing the same title, plus about fifty more. Half are concerned with cowboy life. Most have a line of music. Also included is the interesting collector's note written by John A. Lomax for the 1910 edition.

Cowboy and Western Songs: A Comprehensive Anthology. Austin E. Fife and Alta S. Fife. Music editor, Mary Jo Schwab. New York: Clarkson N. Potter, Bramhall House, 1969. Approximately one-third of this collection of 128 songs is devoted to the cowboy, the remainder to nesters, outlaws, California gold seekers. It includes three strays from the western fringes of Tin Pan Alley—"Steamboat Bill," "Red Wing," and "Ragtime Cowboy Joe." Each song has a line of music and brief headnotes. A sixteen-page lexicon explains western terms that may not be familiar to the reader.

Cowboy Lore. Jules Verne Allen. San Antonio: Naylor Co., 1971. This virtually unchanged reprint of a book Allen first published in 1933 contains thirty-six songs with piano accompaniment. It is one of the few collections to include a variant of "The Santa Fe Trail," words by James Grafton Rogers, music by J. H. Gower, issued in sheet music in 1911 by the Comet Publishing Company of Denver. Allen, Texas born and a working cowpuncher before he became a radio personality and a Victor recording artist, also describes the cowboy's clothing and gear, explains cattle brands and earmarks, and offers a brief dictionary of western words.

The Hell-Bound Train: A Cowboy Songbook. Glenn Ohrlin. Foreword by Archie Green. Biblio-discography by Harlan Daniel. Urbana: University of Illinois Press, 1973. One hundred songs, old, new, and in between, almost all with a western flavor, as sung or collected by Glenn Ohrlin, working cowboy and former rodeo contestant who hangs up his spurs near Mountain View, Arkansas. There are tunes for seventy-three, together with drawings and pithy comments by the compiler.

Songs of the Cowboys, by N. Howard ("Jack") Thorp. Introduction, variants, commentary, notes, and a lexicon by Austin E. Fife and Alta S. Fife. Music editor, Naunie Gardner. New York: Clarkson N. Potter, Bramhall House, 1966. A facsimile reproduction of the first printed collection of American cowboy songs, originally published by Thorp in 1908, is included in this scholarly work. Most of the chapters (one devoted to each of the twenty-three songs) contain one or more melodies with an indication of guitar chords. The book also has a bibliography and a reprint of Thorp's article on song collecting, "Banjo in the Cow Camps," written for the *Atlantic Monthly*, August, 1940.

Heaven on Horseback. Austin E. Fife and Alta S. Fife. Logan: Utah State University Press, 1970. Subtitled *Revivalist Songs and Verse in the Cowboy Idiom*, this collection of forty-nine songs, most with a line of music, includes virtually every cowboy song or poem that mentions Heaven or Hell plus a few, such as Badger Clark's "The Glory Trail," that seem to have no connection with either.

Two collections are aimed primarily at juvenile western song devotees. *Cowboy Jamboree: Western Songs and Lore* by Harold W. Felton (New York: Alfred A. Knopf, 1951) has twenty songs, with simplified musical arrangements by Edward Breck, amusing illustrations by Aldren A. Watson, and historical commentary by the compiler. *Cowboys and the Songs They Sang* by Samuel J. Sackett (New York: William R. Scott, 1967) has fourteen songs, with the simplest of piano accompaniments by Lionel Nowak, historical text by the compiler, and photographs from the Erwin Smith and Charles J. Belden collections.

A good sampling of largely traditional western songs also may be found in many printed collections dealing with American folk music in general. The list of current publications includes three by the Lomaxes: *American Ballads and Folk Songs*, compiled by John A. and Alan Lomax (New York: Macmillan Co., 1934), *The Folk Songs of North America* by Alan Lomax (Garden City, N.Y.: Doubleday & Co., 1960), and *The Penguin Book of American Folk Songs* by Alan Lomax (Baltimore: Penguin Books, 1964). Carl Sandburg's longtime favorite *The American Songbag* (New York: Harcourt, Brace & Co., 1927) still is available in hard covers, as well as in a paperback edition issued in 1955 by Harcourt Brace Jovanovich. In 1972 Charles Scribner's Sons (New York) brought out a paperback reprint of Louise Pound's *American Ballads and Songs*, originally published by the same firm in 1922; the book gives only the words of the songs. *Ballads and Folksongs of the Southwest* by Ethel Moore and Chauncey O. Moore was issued in 1964 by the University of Oklahoma Press (Norman).

Out-of-Print Books

Several unusual collections are no longer issued by their publishers but may be found on the shelves of many public and institutional libraries. Foremost among these are *Songs of the Great American West* compiled by Irwin Silber and Earl Robinson (New York: Macmillan Co., 1967) and *Singing Cowboy* by Margaret Larkin (New York: Alfred A. Knopf, 1931; reissued in paperback by Oak Publications [New York], 1963). The first named contains ninety-two songs, each with melody and guitar chords, one-third with piano accompaniment; there is also historical text and a wealth of interesting old illustrations, as well as a lengthy bibliography and an LP discography. Miss Larkin's volume has forty songs with piano accompaniments, a lengthy introduction, headnotes, and a glossary of cowboy terms.

The second anthology compiled by John A. Lomax, *Songs of the Cattle Trail and Cow Camp* (New York: Macmillan Co., 1919; reissued in 1947 by Duell, Sloan and Pearce [New York]), contains no music; it is chiefly a collection of western verses, many credited to established poets such as Badger Clark, Henry Herbert Knibbs, and James Barton Adams. B. A. Botkin's *A Treasury of Western Folklore* (New York: Crown Publishers, 1951), although primarily a prose dissertation on folklore, contains within its eight hundred pages the words and tunes for nearly fifty western songs and ballads. Twenty-five numbers with piano accompaniment make up *Songs of the West* by Paul Glass and Louis C. Singer (New York: Grosset & Dunlap, 1966).

LP Recordings

In spite of the alleged cowboy costumes that adorn so many performers on record jackets, really good albums of genuine old-time western songs are few in number. The best commercial recordings on the market today are described below; also listed, chiefly for the benefit of collectors, are the better older discs. Whether an album is available from the publisher usually may be determined by consulting the monthly and semiannual Schwann guides on file in larger record shops and many libraries or obtainable from W. Schwann, 137 Newbury Street, Boston, Massachusetts 02116. The companies, of course, have their own catalogues, which generally may be obtained by writing directly to them.

The Archive of Folk Song at the Library of Congress has produced several LPs featuring songs of the cowboys and other inhabitants of the western frontier, such as *Cowboy Songs, Ballads, and Cattle Calls from Texas* (L 28), recorded by John A. Lomax and others between 1941 and 1948. Readers with a scholarly interest in the subject are urged to write for a free phonograph record brochure titled *Folk Recordings*. Address the Library of Congress, Music Division, Recorded Sound Section, Washington, D.C. 20540.

There are at least two collegiate western song recording ventures worthy of mention. In 1964 the Campus Folksong Club at the University of Illinois issued *The Hell-Bound Train* (CFC 301), an LP with seventeen songs plus guitar music and talk by cowboy Glenn Ohrlin of Mountain View, Arkansas; this record is now available, as Puritan 5009, from Dave Samuelson, P. O. Box 946, Evanston, Illinois 60204. The Arizona Friends of Folklore at Northern Arizona University have issued three LPs of local music. Their first record, *Cowboy Songs* (AFF 33–1), released in 1971, has Gail Gardner of Prescott, Arizona, among its varied performers. On the second, *Cowboy Songs, 2* (AFF 33–2), Bill Simon of Prescott sings Badger Clark's "Spanish Is the Lovin' Tongue." A third LP, *In an Arizona Town* (AFF 33–3), from 1973, captures songs and fiddle tunes by the citizens of Clay Springs, Arizona. The cowboy song tradition is continued here with "Billy Venero" and a humorous newcomer, "Cowboy's Shirttail." For information write Keith Cunningham, Box 4064, Northern Arizona University, Flagstaff, Arizona 86001.

Two other Arizonans have each recently issued an LP with their favorite western songs—Singin' Sam Agins, Box 3057, West Sedona, Arizona 86340, and "Peso" Dollar of 3228 West Sahuaro Drive, Phoenix, Arizona 85029.

Stanley Floyd Kilarr, 1402 East Main Street, Klamath Falls, Oregon 97601, markets the recordings of Reno's "Nevada Slim" (Dallas Turner) and reissues famous old discs on his Rare Arts label. His lists of these and other available LPs always contain interesting surprises. *Those Fabulous "Beverly Hill Billies"* (Rare Arts Records WLP 1000) carries the first recording of "The Big Corral" and includes a full version of "The Strawberry Roan" sung by "guest star" Nubbins (J. E. Patterson) of the Arizona Wranglers.

High on the list of authentic cowboy song collections issued commercially in recent years are LPs by the late Slim Critchlow, former cowpuncher and National Park Service ranger, the late Tex Ritter, well known as both a singer and an erstwhile actor in Hollywood westerns, cowboy painter and sculptor Harry Jackson, and Glenn Ohrlin.

Critchlow's pleasing voice, good diction, and simple guitar strumming combine to make a real gem of his eighteen-number collection *The Crooked Trail to Holbrook* (Arhoolie 5007), released in 1970. The jacket contains a brief autobiographical sketch and the singer's own notes describing and explaining his selections. This LP is issued by Arhoolie Records (Box 9195, Berkeley, California 94709), Chris Strachwitz's virtual one-man operation.

Veteran entertainer Tex Ritter is in top form with *Chuck Wagon Days* (Capitol ST 213), a 1969 stereophonic recording of ten numbers, most of them familiar for decades to cowboy song buffs. A male chorus joins in from time to time, and the instrumental accompaniments are quite varied. A highlight is Tex's recitation of Badger Clark's famous poem "A Cowboy's Prayer," set against the music of "The Cowboy's Dream" ("Roll on, roll on, roll on, little dogies, roll on, roll on").

Shortly before Tex passed away in early 1974, Capitol Records produced *An American Legend* (SKC–11241), a three-record reissue of his biggest hits, including Curley Fletcher's "Bad Brahma Bull." Of special interest is Tex's added narrative about the songs, his career, and the people whose lives touched his, among them J. Frank Dobie and John Lomax.

Harry Jackson's two-disc album of twenty-nine numbers, *The Cowboy: His Songs, Ballads, and Brag Talk* (Folkways FH 5723), produced in 1961, is for those who can take their cowboy singing in slow tempo and without accompaniment of any kind. Printed song texts included with the discs are an aid to those who may have difficulty with Jackson's gruff style of delivery. Folklorist Kenneth S. Goldstein contributes a biography of the artist-singer, a lengthy discussion of cowboy music, and notes on the various songs.

A decade after his debut on the Campus Folksong Club label, Glenn Ohrlin, with his wife, Kay, has cut a new LP of western selections for Philo Records. Most of the eighteen songs appear in his book, *The Hell-Bound Train*; newcomers include "The Top Hand," "Mexican Tune," and "The Burial of Wild Bill." Glenn also sings "Zebra Dun," "The Tenderfoot" (O'Malley's "The 'D2' Horse Wrangler"), "Santa Fe Trail," and Badger Clark's "High Chin Bob." *Glenn Ohrlin* (Philo 1017) is available from Philo Records, The Barn, North Ferrisburg, Vermont 05473.

In 1965 RCA Victor brought out in its Vintage series *Authentic Cowboys and Their Western Folksongs* (LPV 522), a collection of songs originally recorded for Victor between 1925 and 1934. There are four by Carl T. Sprague, two each by Jules Verne Allen, Harry McClintock, and Powder River Jack and Kitty Lee, with single numbers by six other singers.

During the past few years Folk Variety Records of West Germany has issued an amazing number of LPs of American folk, country, and western music. Included are a disc with sixteen old Jules Allen cowboy songs issued by Victor on 78s, a newly taped collection of fourteen songs by Carl Sprague, and a second Sprague disc with sixteen of his old Victor 78s. For a catalogue, write to Richard Weize, FV Schallplatten, 2800 Bremen, Box 110142, West Germany.

Other LPs by individual singers, most of them in print, are *Frontier Ballads* (Stinson SLPS 18) by Bill Bender; *Songs of the West* (Folkways FH 5259) by Dave Fredrickson; *Cowboy Ballads* (Folkways

FA 2022) by Cisco Houston; *Peter LaFarge Sings of the Cowboys* (Folkways FA 2533); *Songs of the West* (Tradition TLP 2061) by Ed McCurdy; *Sweet Nebraska Land* (Folkways FH 5337) by Roger Welsch; *The Days of '49* (Folkways FH 5255) by Logan English; and *No Letter Today* (RCA Camden CAL 2171) by Wilf Carter.

Group recordings that best reflect the spirit of the Old West are *Songs of the West* (Columbia CL 657) by the Norman Luboff Choir; *Folk Songs of the Frontier* (Capitol P 8332) by the Roger Wagner Chorale; and *Favorite Cowboy Songs* (RCA Victor LPM 1130) by the Sons of the Pioneers.

Columbia's Legacy series includes two elaborate western song albums. One is *Mormon Pioneers* (LL 1023), with fifteen songs. Extra jacket pages carry extensive text on Mormon history and numerous antique photographs. Two discs make up Columbia Legacy series album L21 1011, *The Bad Men*. One has songs, the other stories of western outlaws from the Black Hills to the Mexican border.

For collectors, here are a few more noteworthy titles from earlier days: *Songs of the Saddle* (Columbia HL 9013) by Bob Atcher; *Gold in California* (Riverside RLP 12–654) by Pat Foster with Dick Weissman; *Cow Camp Songs of the Old West* by George Gillespie (privately issued in Scottsdale, Arizona); *Traditional Songs of the Old West* (Stinson SLP 37) by Cisco Houston and Bill Bender; *Songs of the Frontier* by Burl Ives (Album 5 of the Encyclopedia Britannica Film Series issued in the early 1950s); *The Old Chisholm Trail* (Riverside RLP 12–631, also Washington WLP 125) by Merrick Jarrett; *Songs of the Chisholm Trail* (Mercury MG 20008) by Tony Kraber; *Get Along Little Dogies* (Decca DL 5035) by Frank Luther; *Songs of the Old West* (Elektra EKL 112) by Ed McCurdy; *Trail Dust 'n' Saddle Leather* by Ray Oman (Ace Recordings, issued privately at Prineville, Oregon).

Rodeo life is documented in song on two unusual LPs, both made by veteran rodeo contestants. *Songs of the Rodeo* (Audio Arts 705) has a dozen numbers written and sung by Johnny Baker. For those not familiar with rodeo lingo, extensive liner notes explain the songs and the specialized cowboy terms used in many of them. Baker's address is Route 2, Edwards, Missouri 65326. The other LP, *Chris LeDoux Sings of Rodeo Life*, has fewer songs (seven) about the rugged characters who make their living riding bucking broncos and wrestling steers. Four other songs with a western flavor complete the LeDoux collection. For information write to American Cowboy Songs, The Homeplace, Route 2, Mount Juliet, Tennessee 37122.

Appendix B
A John White Discography

Listed below are the twenty songs I put on ten-inch 78 rpm discs for the American Record Corporation during my brief career as a recording artist, which is described at the beginning of this book.

For reasons long forgotten, only three of these songs carried my real name, and just why someone at ARC believed labels with such colorless pseudonyms as Jimmie Price or Whitey Johns would sell more records than those touting radio singer John White, the Lonesome Cowboy, will remain a mystery. Putting fictitious names on platters seems simply to have been something that was in vogue forty-odd years ago. Vernon Dalhart, who recorded some eight hundred songs, had a barrelful of pseudonyms.

In the Introduction I stated that my partner Roy Smeck played guitar for my various recordings. Roy switched to the banjo now and then, played the harmonica, and often supplied sound effects. Other musicians helped out from time to time, as is obvious from the recordings, but at this late date their names escape me. Adelyne Hood, who has the lead part in "Calamity Jane," had previously recorded this novelty number with Dalhart. She also played violin on many of his discs.

Each of the four old-time western songs on the list—"The Little Old Sod Shanty," "Great Grand Dad," "Whoopee-Ti-Yi-Yo," and "Strawberry Roan"—has its own chapter in this book. My ARC recordings of these four numbers, made available by Norm Cohen and Eugene Earle (John Edwards Memorial Foundation) and by Bob Pinson (Country Music Foundation), are also reissued on the accompanying soundsheet, MAL 752.

For much of this discographic information, I am indebted to Chicago record collector Harlan Daniel, with assists from Chris Comber (Bexleyheath, England), Jim Hadfield (Richville, New York), Frank Mare (Fort Lee, New Jersey), Bob Olson (Chehalis, Washington), John R. Owen (Phoenix, Arizona), Alex Robertson (Pointe Claire, Canada), and Tony Russell (London). The recording dates are those in the ARC files, composer credits those on the record labels. The artist names or pseudonyms which appear on the labels are listed preceding the release numbers. The following label abbreviations have been used:

Apex	Apex (Canada)	Linc	Lincoln
Ban	Banner	Mel	Melotone (Canada)
Bdwy	Broadway	Ori	Oriole
Cam	Cameo	Para	Paramount
Chal	Challenge	Pat	Pathe
Conq	Conqueror	Perf	Perfect
Crn	Crown (Canada)	Reg	Regal
Dom	Domino	Rex	Rex (U.K.)
Hstd	Homestead	Rom	Romeo
Imp	Imperial (U.K.)	Roy	Royal (Canada)
Jwl	Jewel		

All the recordings were made in New York City.

MASTER NO.	TITLE	RELEASE NOS.
August 9, 1929		
8923 (1)	"The Little Old Sod Shanty"	Unissued?
8924 (1)	"Great Grand Dad"	Unissued?
September 19, 1929		
8923 (2)	"The Little Old Sod Shanty" (Cameo master no. 4089)	*Jimmie Price*: Rom 1118 ("Little Old Sod Shanty") *Whitey John*: Jwl 5723 *Whitey Johns*: Ban 6532, Bdwy 8132, Cam 9321 (also "My Little Old Sod Shanty"), Chal 840, Conq 7725, Jwl 5723, Para 3190, Rom 1118 *Lone Star Ranger:* Conq 7434, Dom 4440, Imp 2216 ("The Little Old Shanty"), Pat 32488, Perf 12567, Reg 8881 Reissued on MAL 752 and on *Paramount Old Time Tunes*, JEMF 103

MASTER NO.	TITLE	RELEASE NOS.
8924 (2)	"Great Grand Dad" (Cameo master no. 4090)	*Jimmie Price*: Cam 9314, Rom 1105 *Whitey Johns*: Ban 6561, Chal 852 ("Great Grand-Dad"), Jwl 5749 ("Great Grand-Dad"), Ori 1751 *Lone Star Ranger*: Conq 7434, Dom 4440, Pat 32488, Perf 12567, Reg 8881 Reissued on MAL 752

October 12, 1929

9073	"Farm Relief Song" (Cameo master no. 4140) (Smith-[Betsy] White)	*Jimmie Price*: Cam 9315, Linc 3339, Rom 1106 *Whitey Johns*: Ban 6561, Chal 852, Jwl 5749, Ori 1751 *Lone Star Ranger*: Bdwy 8144, Conq 7438, Dom 4442, Para 3208, Pat 32491, Perf 12570, Reg 8885

November 13, 1929

9136	"The Crow Song (Caw Caw Caw)" (Thompson-Guernsey)	*Whitey Johns*: Ban 0556, Cam 0156, Chal 878, Jwl 5810, Ori 1810, Rom 1176 *Lone Star Ranger*: Bdwy 8144, Conq 7466, Conq 7728, Para 3208, Pat 32504, Perf 12583
9137	"The Deserted Cabin" (Bob Miller)	*Whitey Johns*: Ban 0556, Cam 0156, Chal 878, Jwl 5810, Ori 1810, Rom 1176 *Lone Star Ranger*: Conq 7726, Pat 32501, Perf 12580
9138	"When Bill Hilly Plays a Hillbilly Tune"	*Whitey Johns*: Ban 0583, Cam 0183, Hstd 23012, Jwl 5839, Ori 1839, Rom 1205

November 22, 1929

9172	"At Father Power's Grave" (Clarence Gaskill)	*Whitey Johns*: Ban 0560, Cam 0160, Jwl 5812, Ori 1812 *The Old Sexton*: Pat 32501, Perf 12580 *Lone Star Ranger*: Conq 7726
9173	"The Unmarked Grave" (Bob Miller)	*Whitey Johns*: Ban 0560, Cam 0160, Jwl 5812, Ori 1812

December 4, 1929

9203	"The Prison Warden's Secret" (Pearl)	*Whitey Johns*: Ban 0581, Cam 0181, Chal 875, Hstd 16155, Jwl 5837, Ori 1837, Rom 1200

MASTER NO.	TITLE	RELEASE NOS.
		Lone Star Ranger: Bdwy 8141, Conq 7482, Conq 7782, Para 3201, Pat 32510, Perf 12589, Reg 8938
9204	"The Train That Never Arrived"	*Whitey Johns*: Ban 0585, Cam 0185, Jwl 5841, Ori 1841, Rom 1204
		Lone Star Ranger: Bdwy 8142, Para 3202
9205	"Pappy's Buried on the Hill" (Pearl)	*Whitey Johns*: Jwl 5904, Ori 1904
		Lone Star Ranger: Ban 0649, Bdwy 8141 ("My Pappy's Buried on the Hill"), Cam 0249, Conq 7482, Conq 7782, Jwl 5904, Ori 1904, Para 3201, Pat 32510, Perf 12589, Reg 8938, Rom 1268
		The Lonesome Cowboy: Ban 0649

January 23, 1930

9302	"I'm Just a Black Sheep" (Henry Ainsworth Dawson)	*Whitey Johns*: Ban 0618, Cam 0218, Jwl 5875, Ori 1875, Rom 1237
		Lone Star Ranger: Apex 41152, Conq 7492, Crn 81365, Dom 4509, Mel 81365, Perf 12591, Reg 8954
		The Lonesome Cowboy: Perf 12591
9303	"Hillbilly Courtship" (Bob Miller)	*Whitey Johns*: Ban 0617, Cam 0217, Hstd 23016, Jwl 5873, Ori 1873, Rom 1235

February 5, 1930

9340	"Calamity Jane" [duet with Adelyne Hood] (Fields-Hall)	*Adelyne Hood*: Ban 0645, Cam 0245, Conq 7500, Jwl 5900, Ori 1900, Perf 12594, Reg 8955, Rom 1261
9341	"Eleven More Months and Ten More Days" (Fields-Hall)	*Whitey Johns*: Hstd 16065, Jwl 5904, Ori 1904
		Lone Star Ranger: Apex 41170, Ban 0649, Bdwy 8150, Cam 0249, Chal 877, Conq 7509, Conq 7727, Crn 81354, Imp 2274, Imp 2602, Jwl 5904, Mel 12106, Ori 1904, Para 3218, Perf 12598, Reg 8973, Rom 1268
		Frank Ranger: Rex 8056
		The Lonesome Cowboy: Ban 0649, Conq 7727, Perf 12598

MASTER NO.   TITLE   RELEASE NOS.

March 31, 1930

9539   "Take Care of the   *Whitey Johns*: Ban 0682, Jwl 5935,
            Farmer"   Ori 1935
            (Gaskill)   *Lone Star Ranger*: Ban 0682, Cam 0282,
                                      Conq 7549
                                      The Lonesome Cowboy: Perf 12616

9540 (1) "The Prisoner's   Unissued?
            Rosary"

April 14, 1930

9540 (2) "The Prisoner's   *Whitey Johns*: Chal 895, Jwl 5964,
            Rosary"   Ori 1964, Reg 10019
            (Clarence Gaskill)   *Lone Star Ranger*: Ban 0707, Cam 0307,
                                      Conq 7603, Perf 12637
                                    The Lonesome Cowboy: Perf 12637

April 2, 1931

10541   "Whoopee-Ti-Yi-Yo *John White (The Lonesome Cowboy)*:
           (Git Along Little   Ban 32179, Conq 7753, Mel 91249,
           Doggies [*sic*])"   Ori 8066, Perf 12709, Perf 12712,
                                    Rom 1629 ("Little Doggie"), Rom
                                    5066, Roy 91249 ("Little Doggie")
                                    Reissued on MAL 752

10542   "Strawberry Roan" *John White (The Lonesome Cowboy)*:
           [Curley Fletcher   Conq 7753, Perf 12712, Roy 91249
           version]   Reissued on MAL 752

April 16, 1931

10571   "Strawberry Roan" *John White (The Lonesome Cowboy)*:
           (Howard-Vincent)   Ban 32179, Mel 91249, Ori 8066,
                                    Perf 12709 [master no. given as
                                    10542], Rom 1629 [master no. given
                                    as 10542], Rom 5066

Index